THE ANCIENT'S BOOK OF MAGIC

An historical record of the secret procedures
and practices of the ancient masters and adepts

by

LEWIS de CLAREMONT

Author of

The Ancient's Book Of Magic
The Master's Course Of Lessons In Hypnotism
Legends Of Incense, Herb And Oil Magic
The Home Herb Doctor
Secrets Of Attraction
How To Get Your Winning Number
The Ten Lost Books Of The Prophets
The Seven Keys To Power
Inventor Of Hypnopoule

*"The deeper the mind penetrates, the clearer it becomes, the more it
spreads itself out on the surface, the more it is confused."*

*"Read less, think more of what you have read, act towards a difficult
task as a brave general who leaves his foe no rest till he has overthrown
him."*

—*Confucius*

PUBLISHED BY

DORENE PUBLISHING CO.

1353 FULTON STREET
BROOKLYN, NEW YORK 11216

INTRODUCTION

After many years of intensive research into the mysterious and hidden arts of invocation, I have finally compiled this book, which, I feel, will be my greatest book on an art that has long been lost and which, at one time, served to give the magician and occult devotee the office of guardian of the invisible forces.

It has long been my contention that the story of Alladin's Lamp has often been interpreted thusly: that the Alladin's Lamp was a mere instrument or an incident in the invocator's ritual and accessory; an instrument by which the compack of invocation can be selected. To many of my "Chelas" (students) have I told that the historical story of Alladin was falsely interpreted by our historians and that the true significance of the Alladin's Lamp was basically mystical and that the invocator had merely to rub the soul of the Lamp to invoke the genii.

The devoted student of occultism and the mere curiosity-seeker may both differ in the adherence to the rituals that I will set forth just as I have interpreted them from the ancients. Those of you who seek only to gain success, may gain it—but the great result will be, for it is surely written **"That he who uses the works of the magician falsely, shall himself be falsely accused."**

In the following pages you will find many ways that I have invoked very many different Spirits, Demons, Angels and Goblins. I implore you; those of you who will attempt the invocation of either good or bad Demons, Spirits, Angels or Goblins to do so with the greatest amount of self-respect and confidence. For, I have found in many years of experience that those who supply the actions of God be not seriously considering the strain. Of the many invocations included, you will find them as an analysis of the great Solar Intelligences, and interpretation leading to an awareness and complete appreciation.

5

Let me, at this point, pause and go into what I think the uses of so many of our friends are desirous—of this hidden knowledge which I feel has been revealed for the first time. In ancient times, there is record that certain mystics invoked many a spirit to do his bidding. Some historical records show that Cleopatra compelled an enemy to lose his power to harm her and forced him to become a slave and lover, by her magical use of scented oils and sorcery. At this time a great cult in Egypt was a sacred and mystic legion in which Isis and Asoris were Deities. The practitioners and priest in this cult, by a high invocation, were said, able to leave the body and ascend to the 7th Heaven to make compacks with Isis, the Immortal of immortals. As the story is told, this son of a high priest was sent to use his magical art in forcing the help and consent of Cleopatra to the aid of his secret order. By her great sorcery, she conjured the forces of a great demon which destroyed his power and caused him to become her slave. When the great priests of the order learned of this, they immediately induced high and mighty invocations and commanded demons and goblins, and secondary spirits of evil and lust, to wreck her whole kingdom which is shown to us by historical account of the fall of Cleopatra by her own hands.

Shakespeare, in the play 'The Tempest," clearly reveals that in the Elizabethan Age the work of the invocator and conjurer was understood, and its art practiced with great zeal. For Ariel, a great demon, it is said, was invoked by the Duke of Milan to cause the destruction of his enemy who had banished him to a desert island.

From the earliest times, we have found traces of the many uses of invocations that are hidden to the untrained eye but vividly clear to the invocating magician. Many historians, occult and otherwise, have shown us that such men as Gilles de Retz, Robert Owen, Dr. Hodgson, Joan of Arc, Swedenberg acquired great wealth, riches, friends, and power by invocating certain demons, spirits, goblins, and angels to do their bidding. There are few limitations to the possibilities of the attainment of the spirits, demons, goblins and angels, for they are bound by a force mightier than might to carry out the biddings of those that invoke them.

There is no dimension limiting them, nor is there any finite time. Theirs is the power of the ultimate consciousness.

I, do hereby say, without fear of an contradiction, that it has been revealed to me through many, many years of research that the ancients have invoked many of the demons, goblins, angels and spirits to do their bidding and I sincerely believe that today, to the gifted and the earnest and the fearless and the pure, the hidden powers of magic is still open.

The person who seeks love, luck, success, riches, prosperity, gold, treasures, lost ones, etc. can, if they desire, by following the acts of the ancients, tread their mystical patheways in accomplishing the seemingly impossible things to their greatest advantage. For knowing that a spirit, demon or a goblin properly invoked—must carry out the bidding of his invocator. The limitations of the invocator's demand are very small and it is my belief that, with a proper understanding and carrying out of the instructions, any person may be able to invoke any spirit, demon or goblin at his command.

LEWIS DE CLAREMONT

CHAPTER 1

SECRET PROCEDURE IN ORDER TO MAKE AN INVOCATION

First, from the list contained herein, choose a spirit, demon, goblin or angel, or a spirit of a friend or close relative, set a day for invocating them and prepare in the following manner: a day prior to the invocation shall be devoted to a fast. for 24 hours, the person must take no liquid or solid food. As the hour approaches, set by the magician for the invocation, all mirrors should be covered by white cloth, and all glass shall be covered. Anything that might reflect a living thing and not a living thing should be covered for spirits, demons, goblins and angels feel offended when a shining thing is placed in front of them and they do not see themselves in it.

Now, 3 hours before the time set for the invocation, the invocator burns the incense desired. This is found numbered besides the name of the spirit listed on the back of the book. He then moves all furniture to the sides of the room, leaving a clearance in the center, removing all rugs and cloths from the floor so that nothing but the bare floor can be seen. Then, making a huge circle, about 3 to 4 feet in diameter with chalk, preferably Dragon's Blood Brand Chalk, he writes the holy words: Tetragramaton and writes his own name and the name of father and the name of his mother in the circle. Placing the incense also in the circle and lighting 2 candles on both sides of the incense, the color designated in the list, he then lets them burn for 12 minutes to show the light, then extinquishes the lights from the candles and lets the incense burn and removes to the bathroom. Here he bathes, after having placed an amount of sanctuary oil in the tub. After having bathed himself and anointed himself pleasingly with oils, he rubs his forehead with powder which will later be given. Then he dresses himself placing the Tsitsus close to his body, and puts on his regular clothes and places the invocator's gown over them. The tails, he puts on top of them and binds his head and forehead with the Phylectary.

He then takes the stick and walks to the room where he has drawn the circle and enters into the circle. Once he enters into the circle with his books, wands , incense and all things he needs, he draws the outer circle about 3 inches away from the circle he has already drawn and in it he then lights the candles, sprays the perfume and re-lights the incense and opens to the first invocation as contained in the book. The operator must remember not to leave this circle during the whole invocation until the closing words have been said, for as long as he remains in the circle, no matter how fierce the demons may be they cannot break through the walls of the circle, for they are bound and protected by the fiery pillars of Jericno and he is protected by the Legion of 72 who form a protecting ring around the circle whence no one can force their way through, in defense of the consequence of the Higher Intelligence.

Spirits are said to be attracted by certain colored candles. In fact, it is considered by the adepts of the past, the aim of the color spectrum transients magnetic vibrations of tremendous force, consult the list for the proper color candle that is sympathetic to each spirit. In making the invocation, the desires of the invocator must be written on parchment and read to the demon, spirit or goblin out loud. A huge stick must be had to subdue the demon or goblin by constantly banging the stick on the floor in order to subdue them. Then when they are subdued, the invocator should have the spirit return on the following day or some day when they are ready to go out to do the biddings, and on a day at a certain place with a certain book, the invocator reads the desires to the demon, spirit or goblin from virgin parchment, and by invocating the high and mighty name of God: Tetragramaton, Adenoi, etc. Commence then to carry out this written, sealed and signed order. Thus, they cannot refuse the request of the invocator and must carry out their biddings, whether they be good or evil. But we warn the embryo magician to beware of the consequences of evil. The Lord's retribution is inevitable. "What ye sow, so shall ye reap."

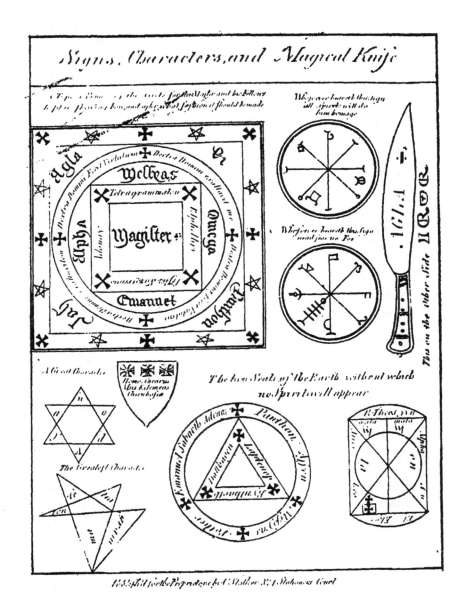

MAGICAL DIAGRAMS AND REQUISITES

CHAPTER II

THE MAGICAL ART OF NECROMANCY

Necromancy, ordivination by means of the spirits of the dead, from the Greek words, **nekros**, dead; and **manteia**, devination. It is through its Italian from **nigromancia**, that it came to be known as the "Black Art." With the Greeks it originally signified the descent into Hades in order to consult the dead rather than summonsing the dead into the mortal sphere again. The art is of almost universal usage. Considerable difference of opinion exists among modern adepts as to the exact methods to be properly pursued in the necromatic art, and it must be borne in mind that necromancy, which in the Middle Ages was called sorcery, shades into modern spiritualistic practice. There is no doubt however, that necromancy is the touch-stone of occultism, for if, after careful preparation the adept can carry through to a successful issue, the raising of the soul from the other world, he has proved the value of his art. It would be fruitless in this place to enter into a psychological discussion as to whether this feat is possible of accomplishment or not, and we will confine ourselves to the material which has been placed at our disposal by the sages of the past, who have left full details as to how the process should be approached.

In the case of a compact existing between the conjuror and the devil, no ceremony is necessary, as the familiar is ever at hand to do the behests of his masters. This, however, is never the case with the true sorcerer, who preserves his independence and trusts to his profound knowledge of the art and his powers of command. His object, therefore, is to "constrain" some spirit to appear before him, and to guard himself from the danger of provoking such beings. The magician, it must be understood, always has an assistant, and every article named is prepared according to rules well known in the black art. In the first place they are to fix upon a proper spot for such a purpose; which must be either in a subterranean vault, hung round with black, and lighted by a magical torch; or else in the centre of some thick wood or desert, or upon some extensive unfrequented plain, where several roads meet, or amidst the ruins of ancient castles, abbeys, monasteries, etc., or amongst the rocks on the sea shore, in some private detached churchyard, or any other solemn, melancholy place between the hours of twelve and one in the night, either when the moon shines very bright, or else when the elements are disturbed with storms of thunder, lightning, wind, and rain: for, in these places, time, and seasons, it is contended that spirits can with less difficulty manifest themselves to mortal eyes, and continue visible with the least pain, in the elemental external world.

When the proper time and place is fixed upon, a magic circle is to be formed, within which the master and his associate are carefully to retire. The dimensions of the circle are as follows: A piece of ground is usally chosen, nine feet share, at the full extent of which parallel lines are drawn one within the other, having sundry crosses and triangles described between them, close to which is formed the first or outer circle, then about half-a-foot within the same, a second circle is described and within that another square correspondent to the first, the centre of which is the seat or spot where the master and associate are to be placed. "The vacancies formed by the various lines and angles of the figure are filled up with the holy names of God, having crosses and triangles described between them. The reason assigned by magicians and others for the institution and use of circles, is, that so much ground being blessed and consecrated by such holy words and ceremonies as they make use of in forming it, hath a secret force to expell all evil spirits from the bounds thereof, and, being sprinkled with pure sanctified water the ground is purified from all uncleaness; besides, the holy names of God being written over every part of it, its force becomes so powerful that no evil spirit hath ability to break through it or to get at the magician or his companion, by reason of the antipathy in nature they bear to these sacred names. And the reason given for the triangles, is, that the spirit be not easily brought to speak the truth, they may by the exorcist conjured to enter the same, where, by virtue of the names of the essence and divinity of God, they can speak nothing but what is true and right. The circle, therefore, according to this account of it, is the principal fort and shield of the magician, from which he is not, at the peril of his life, to depart till he has completely dismissed the spirit, particularly if he be of a fiery or internal nature. Tradition records many instances of those who perished by this means; particularly the legend of "Chiancungi," the famous Egyptian fortune-teller, who was so famous in England in the 17th century. He undertook for a wager, to raide up the spirit "Bokim," and having described the circle, he seated his sister Napula by him as his associate. After frequently repeating the forms of exorcism, and calling upon the spirit to appear, and nothing as yet answering his demand, they grew impatient of the business, and quitted the circle, but it cost them their lives; for they were instantaneously seized and crushed to death by that infernal spirit, who happened not to be sufficiently constrained till that moment, to manifest himself to human eyes."

There is a prescribed form of consecrating the magic circle, which we have illustrated later on. The proper attire or "pontificalibus" of a magician, is an Ephod made of fine white linen, over that a priestly robe of black Bombazine, reaching to the ground, with the two seals of the earth drawn correctly upon virgin parchment, and affixed to a broad consecrated girdle, with the names, Ya, Ya,—Aie, Aaie,—Elibra,—Elchim, — Sadai, — Pah Adonai, — two robore,—Cinctus sum. Upon his shoes must be written Tetragramation, with crosses round about; upon his a high-crowned cap of silk, and in his hand a Holy Bible, printed or written in pure Hebrew. Thus attired, and standing within the charmed circle, the magician repeats the awful form of exorcism; and presently, the infernal spirits make strange and frightful noises, howlings, tremblings, flashes, and most dreadful shrieks and yells, as the forerunner becomes visible. Their first appearance is generally in the form of fierce and terrible lions or tigers, vomiting forth fire, and roaring hideously about the circle; all which the time the exorcist must not suffer any tremour of dismay; for, in that case, they will gain the ascendency and the consequences may touch his life. On the contrary, he must summon up a share of resolution, and continue repeating all the forms of construction and confinement until they are drawn nearer to the influence of the triangle, when their forms will change to appearances less ferocious and frightful, and become

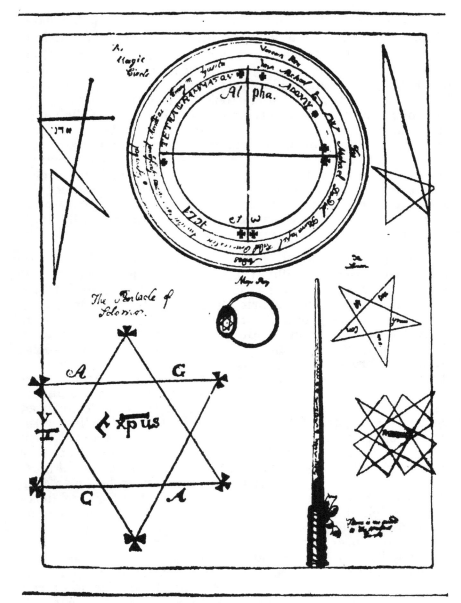

ANOTHER MAGIC CIRCLE AND PENTACLE OF SOLOMON

more submissive and tractable. When the forms of conjuration have in this manner been sufficiently repeated, the spirits forsake their bestial shapes, and enter the human form appearing like naked men of gentle countenance and behaviour, yet is the magician to be warily on his guard that they deceive him not by such mild gestures, for they are exceedingly fraudulent and deceitful in their dealings with those who constrain them to appear without compact, having nothing in view but to suborn his mind, or accomplish his destruction. With great care also must the spirit be discharged after the ceremony is finished, and he has answered all the demands made upon him. The magician must wait patiently till the spirit passed through all the terrible forms which announce his coming, and only when the last shriek has died away, and every trace of fire and brimstone has disappeared, may he leave the circle and depart home in safety.

If the ghost of a deceased person is to be raised, the grave must be resorted to at midnight, and a different form of conjuration is necessary. Still another, is the infernal sacrament for "any corpse that hath hanged, drowned, or otherwise made away with itself; "and in this case the conjurations are performed over the body, which will at last arise, and standing upright, answer with a faint and hollow voice the questions that are put to it.

Eliphas Levi, in his Ritual of Transcendental Magic says that "evocations should always have a motive and a becoming end, otherwise they are works of darkness and folly, dangerous for health and reason." The permissible motive of an evocation may be either love or intelligence. Evocations of love require less apparatus and are in every respect easier. The procedure is as follows: "We must, in the first place, carefully collect the memorials of him (or her) whom we desire to behold, the articles he used, and on which his impression remains: we must also prepare an apartment in which the person lived or otherwise one of a similiar kind, and place his portrait veiled in white therein, surrounded with his favourite flowers, which must be renewed daily. A fixed date must then be observed, either the birthday of the person, or the day which was most fortunate for his and our own affection, one of which we may believe that his soul, however blessed elsewhere, cannot lose the remembrance; this must be the day for the evocation, and we must provide for it during the space of fourteen days. Throughout this period we must refrain from extending to anyone the same proofs of affection which we have the right to expect from the dead; we must observe strict chastity, live in retreat, and take only one modest and light collection daily. Every evening at the same hour we must shut ourselves in the chamber consecrated to the memory of the lamented person, using only one small light, such as that of a funeral lamp or taper. This light should be placed behind us, the portrait should be uncovered and we should remain before it for an hour, in silence; finally we should fumigate the apartment with a little good incense, and go out backwards. On the morning of the day fixed for the evocation, we should adorn ourselves as if for a festival, not salute anyone first, make but a single repast of bread, wine, and roots, or fruits; the cloth should be white, two covers should be laid, and one portion of the bread broken should be set aside; a little wine should also be placed in the glass of the person we design to invoke. The meal must be eaten alone in the chamber of evocations, and in presence of the veiled portrait; it must be all cleared away at the end, except the glass belonging to the dead person, and his portion of bread, which must be placed before the portrait. In the evening, at the hour for the regular visit, we must repair in silence to the chamber, light a clear fire of Oak Bark, and cast incense seven times thereon, pronouncing the name of the person whom we desire to behold. The lamp must then be extinguished and the fire permitted to die out. On this day the portrait must not be unveiled. When the flame is extinct, put more incense on the ashes, and invoke God according to the forms of the religion to which the dead person belonged, and according to the ideas which he himself possessed of God. While making this prayer we must identify ourselves with the evoked person, speak as he spoke, believe in a sense as he believed; then, after a silence of fifteen minutes, we must speak to him as if he were present, with affection and with faith, praying him to manifest to us. Renew this prayer mentally, covering the face with both hands; then call him thrice with a loud voice; tarry on our knees, the eyes closed and covered for some minutes; then call again thrice upon him in a sweet and affectionate tone, and slowly open the eyes. Should nothing result, the same experiment must be renewed in the following year, and if necessary a third time, when it is certain that the desired apparition will be obtained and the longer it has been delayed the more realistic and striking it will be.

"Evocations of knowledge and intelligence are made with more solemn ceremonies. If concerned with a celebrated personage, we must meditate for twenty-one days upon his life and writings, form an idea of his appearance, converse with him mentally, and imagine his answers; carry his portrait, or at least his name, about us; follow a vegetable diet for twenty-one days, and a severe fast during the last seven. We must next construct the magical oratory. This oratory must be invariably darkened; but we operate in the daytime, we may leave a narrow aperture on the side where the sun will shine at the hour of the evocation and place a triangular prism before the opening, and a crystal glove, filled with water, before the prism. If the operation be arranged for the night the magic lamp must be so placed that its single ray shall upon the altar smoke. The purpose of the preparations is to furnish the magic agent with elements of corporeal appearance, and to ease as much as possible the tension of imagination, which could not be exalted without danger into the absolute illusion of dream. For the rest, it will be easily understoond that a beam of sunlight, or the ray of a lamp,. coloured variously, and falling upon curling and irregular smoke, can in no way create a perfect image. The chafing-dish containing the sacred fire should be in the center of the oratory, and the altar of perfumes close by. The operator must turn towards the east to pray, and the west to invoke; he must be either alone or assisted by one or two persons perserving the strictest silence; he must wear the magical vestments, which we have described. He should bathe before the operation, and all his undergarments must be of the most intact and scrupulous cleanliness. The ceremony should begin with a prayer suited to the genius of the spirit about to be invoked and one which would be approved by himself if he still lived. For example, it woud be impossible to evoke Voltaire by reciting prayers in the style of St. Bridget. For the great men of anti-

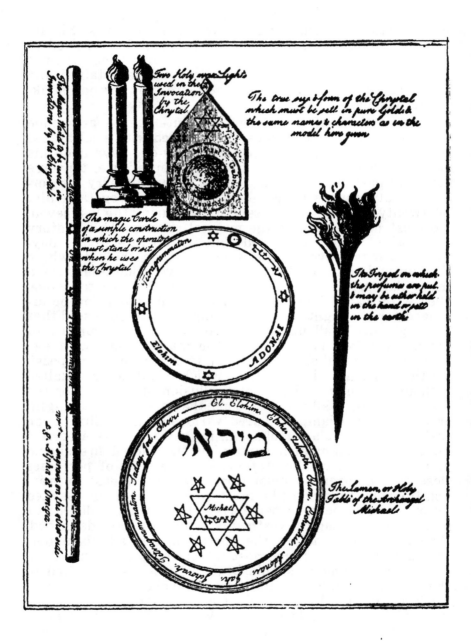

The Magic Wand to be used in Invocations by the Chrystal.

The letters to engraven on the other ends e.g. Alpha et Omega.

Two Holy wax Lights used in the Invocation by the Chrystal

The true size & form of the Chrystal which must be sett in pure Gold & the same names & characters as in the model here given

The magic Circle of a simple construction in which the operator must stand or sit when he uses the Chrystal

The Tripod on which the perfumes are put. It may be either held in the hand or sett in the earth.

The Lamen, or Holy Table of the Archangel Michael

quity, we may see the hymns of Cleanthes or Orpheus, with the adjuration terminating the Golden Verses of Fythagoras. In our own evocation of Apollonious, we used the magical philosophy of Patricius for the ritual, containing the doctrines of Zoroaster and the writing of Hermes Thrismegistus. We recited the Nuctemeron of Apollonious in Greek with a loud voice and add the following conjuration:

"Vouchsafe to be present, O Father of all, and thou Thrice Mighty Hermes, Conductor of the Dead. Asclepius, son of Hephaistus, Patron of the Healing Art; and thou Osiris, Lord of strength and vigour, do thou thyself be present too. A nebascenis, Patron of Philosophy, and yet again Asclepius, son of Imuthe, who presidest over poetry.

"Apollonius, Apollonius, Apollonius, Thou teaches the Magic of Zoroaster, son of Oromasdes; and this is the worship of the Gods." For the evocation of spirits belonging to religions issued from Judaism, the following kabalistic invocation of Solomon should be used, either in Hebrew, or in any other tongue with which the spirit in question is known to have been familiar:—"Powers of the Kingdom, be ye under my left foot and in my right hand! Glory and Eternity, take me by the shoulders, and direct me in the paths of victory! Mercy and Justice, be ye the equilibrium and splendour of my life! Intelligence and Wisdom, crown me! Spirits of Malchuth, lead me betwixt the two pillars upon which rests the whole edifice of the temple! Angels of Netsah and Hod, strengthen me upon the cubic stone of Jesod! O Gedulael! O Geburael! O Tipherth! Binaiel, be thou my love! Ruach Hochmeal, be thou my light! Be that which art and thou shalt be, O Ketheriel! Tschim, assist me in the name of Saddai! Cherubim, be my strength in the name of Adonai! Beni-Elonim, be my brethen in the name of the Son, and by the power of Aebaoth! Elohim, do battle for me in the name of Tetragramaton! Malachim, protect me in the name of Jod He Vau He! Seraphim, cleanse my love in the name of Elvoh! Hasmalim, enlighten me with the Splendours of Eloi and Schechinah Aralim, act! Ophanim, revolve and shine: Hajoth a Kadosh, cry, speak, roar, bellow! Kadosh, Kadosh, Kadosh, Saddai, Adonai, Jotchavah, Eieazereie: Hallelu-jah, Hallelu-jah, Hallelu-jah, Amen.

It should be remembered above all, in conjurations, that the names of Satan, Bellezebub, Adramelek, and others do not designate spiritual unities, but legions of impure spirits. "Our name is legion, for we are many," says the spirit of darkness in the Gospel. Number constitutes the law, and progress takes place inversely in hell—that is to say, the most advanced in Satanic development, and consequently the most degraded, are the least intelligent and feeblest. Thus, a fatal law drives the demons downward when they wish and believe themselves to be ascending. Also those who term themselves chiefs are the most impotent and despised of all. As to the horde of perverse spirits, they tremble before and unknown, invisible, incomprehensible, capricious, implacable chief, who never complains his law, whose arm is ever stretched out to strike those who fail to understand him. They give this phantom the names of Baal, Jupiter, and even others more venerable, which cannot, without profanation, be pronounced in hell. But this Phantom is only a shadow and remnant of God, disfigured by their wilful perversity, and persisting in their imagination like a vengeance of justice, and a remorse of truth.

"When the evoked spirit of light manifests with dejected or irritated countenance, we must offer him a moral sacrifice, that is, be inwardly disposed to renounce whatever offends him; and before leaving the oratory, we must dismiss him, saying: "May peace be with thee! I have not wished to trouble thee: do thou torment me not. I shall labour to improve myself as to anything that vexes thee. I pray, and will still pray, with thee for thee. Pray thou also both with and for me, and return to thy great slumber, expecting that day when we shall wake together. Silence and adieu!"

Christian in his Historie de le Magie (Paris, 1871) says:—"The place chosen for the evocation is not an unimportant point. The most auspicious is undoubetedly that room which contains the vast traces of the lamented person. If it be impossible to fulfill this condition, we must go in search of some isolated rural retreat which corresponds in orientation and aspect, as well as measurement with the mortuary chamber.

"The window must be blocked with boards of olive wood, hermetically joined, so that no exterior light may penetrate. The ceiling, the four interior walls and the floor must be draped with tapestry of emerald green silk, which the operator must himself secure with copper nails, invoking no assistance from strange hands, because, from this moment, he alone may enter into this spot set apart from all, the arcane Oratory of the Magus. The furniture which belonged to the deceased, his favorite possessions and trinkets, the things on which his final glance may be supposed to have rested—all these must be assiduously collected and arranged in order which they occupied at the time of his death. If none of these souvenirs can be obtained, a faithful likeness of the departed being must at least be procured, it must be full length, and must be depicted in the dress and colours which he wore during the last period of his life. This portrait must be set up on the eastern wall by means of copper fasteners, must be covered with a veil of white silk, and must be surmounted with a crown of those flowers which were most loved by the deceased.

"Before this portrait there must be erected an altar of white marble, supported by four columns which must terminate in bull's beet. A five-pointed star must be emblazoned on the slab of the altar, and must be composed of pure copper plates; the place in the centre of the star, between the plates, must be large enough to receive the pedestal of a cup-shaped copper chafing-dish, containing dessicated fragments of laurel wood and alder. By the side of the chafing-dish must be placed a censer full of incense. The skin of a white and spotless ram must be stretched beneath the altar, and on it must be emblazoned another pentagram drawn with parallel lines of azure blue, golden yellow, emerald green, and purple red.

"A copper tripod must be erected in the middle of the Oratory; it must be perfectly triangular in form, it must be surmounted by another and similar chafing-dish which must likewise contain a quantity of dried olive wood.

"A high candelabrum of copper must be placed by the wall on the southern side, and must contain a single taper of purest white wax, which must alone illuminate the mystery of the evocation.

"The white colour of the altar, of the ram's skin, and of the veil, is consecrated to Gabriel, the planetary archangel of the moon, and the Genius of mysteries; the green of the copper and the tapestries is dedicated to the Genius of Venus.

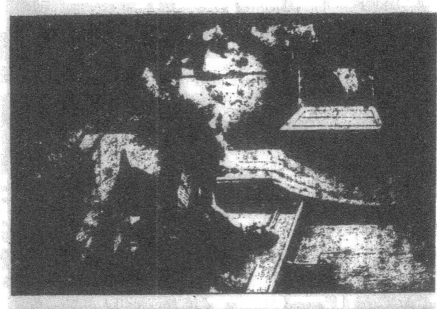

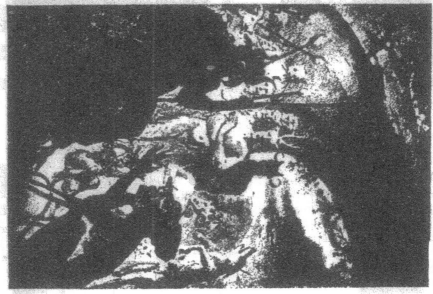

"The altar and tripod must both be encompassed by a magnetized iron chain, and by three garland composed of the foliage and blossoms of the myrtle, the olive and the rose.

"Finally, facing the portrait, and on the eastern side, there must be a canopy, also draped with silk, and supported by two triangular columns of olive wood, plated with purest copper. On the North and South sides, between each of these columns and the wall, the tapestry, must fall in long folds to the ground, forming a kind of tabernacle; which must be open on the eastern side. At the foot of each column there must be a sphinx and a dish with a cavity at the top of the head to receive spices for burning. It is beneath this canopy that the apparitions will manifest, and it should be remembered that Hagus must turn to the east for prayer and to the west for evocation.

"Before entering this little sanctuary devoted to the religion of remembrance, the operator must be clothed in his vestment. On his breast must be the talisman of Venus depending from a ribbon of azure silk.

"The Oratory and all its objects must be consecrated on a Friday, during the hours which are set apart to the Genius of Venus. This consecration is performed by burning violets and roses in a fire of olive wood. A shaft must be provided in the Oratory for the Passage of the smoke, but care must be taken to prevent the admission of light through this channel.

"When these preparations are finished, the operator must impose on himself a retreat of one and twenty days, beginning on the anniversary of the death of the beloved being. During this period he must refrain from conferring on any one the least of those marks of affection which he was accustomed to bestow on the departed; he must be absolutely chaste, alike in deed and thought; he must take daily but one repast, consisting of bread, wine, roots and fruits. These three conditions are indispensable to success in evocation and their accomplishment requires comlpete isolation.

"Every day, shortly before mid-night, the Magus must assume his consecrated dress. On the stroke of the mystic hour, he must enter the Oratory, bearing a lighted candle in his right hand, and in the other an hour-glass. The candle must be fixed in the candelabra, and the hour-glass on

25

the altar to register the flight of time. The operator must then proceed to replenish the garland, and the floral crown. Then he shall unveil the portrait, and erect it immovable in front of the altar, being thus with his face to the East, he shall softly go over in his mind the cherished recollections he possesses of the beloved and departed being.

"When the upper reservoir of the hour-glass is empty the time of contemplation will be over. By the flame of the taper the operator must then kindle the laurel wood and alder in the chafing-dish which stands on the altar; then, taking a pinch of incense from the censer, let him cast it thrice upon the fire, repeating the following words:—"Glory be to the Father of life universal in the splendour of the infinite altitude, and peace in the twilight of the immeasurable depths to all Spirits of good will."

"Then he shall cover the portrait, and taking up his candle in his hand, shall depart from the Oratory, walking backward at a slow pace as far as the threshold. The same ceremony must be fulfilled at the same hour during every day of the retreat, and at each visit the crown which is above the portrait, and the garlands of the altar and tripod must be carefully renewed. The withered leaves and flowers must be burnt each evening in a room adjoining the Oratory.

"When the solemn hour of the evening has at length ar- must do his best to have no communication with any one. but if this be impossible, he must not be the first to speak, and he must postpone all business till the morrow. On the stroke of noon he must arrange a small circular table in the Oratory, and cover it with a new napkin of unblemished whiteness. It must be garnished with two copper chalices, and entire loaf, and a crystal flagon of the purest wine. The bread must be broken and not cut, and the wine emptied in equal portions into the two cups. Half of this mystic communion, which must be his sole nourishment on this supreme day, shall be offered by the operator to the dead, and by the light of the one taper he must eat his own share, standing before the veiled portrait. Then he shall retire as before, walking backward as far as the threshold, and leaving the ghost's share of the bread and wine upon the table.

"When the solemn hour of the evening has at length arrived the Magus shall carry into the Oratory some well-dried cypress wood, which he shall set alight on the altar and the tripod. Three pinches of incense shall be cast on the altar flame in honour of the Supreme Potency which manifests itself by Ever Active Intelligence and by Absolute Wisdom. When the wood of the two chafing-dishes has been reduced to embers, he must renew the triple offering of incense on the altar, and must cast some seven times on the fire in the tripod; at each evaporation of the consecrated perfume he must repeat the previous doxology, and then turning to the East, he must call upon God by the prayer of that religion which has professed by the person whom he desires to evoke.

"When the prayers are over he must reverse his position and with his face to the West, must enkindle the chafing-dishes on the head of each dish, and when the red oak is fully ablaze he must heap over it well-dried violets and roses. Then let him extinquish the candle which illuminates the Oratory, and falling on his knees before the canopy, between the two columns. let him mentally address the beloved person with a plenitude of faith and affection. Let him solemnly entreat it to appear and renew this interior adjuration seven times under the auspices of the seven providential Genii, endeavouring during the whole of the time to exalt his soul above the natural weakness of humanity.

"Finally, the operator, with closed eyes, and with hands covering his face, must call the invoked person in a loud but gentle voice, pronouncing three times all the names which he bore.

Some moments after the third appeal, he must extend his arms in the form of a cross, and lifting up his eyes, he will behold the beloved being in a recognizable manner in front of him. That is to say, he will perceive that ethereal substance separated from the perishable terrestrial body, the fluidic envelope of the soul, which Kabalistic initiates have termed the Perispirit. This substance preserves the human form but is emancicated from human infirmities, and is energised by the special characteristics whereby the imperishable individuality of our essence is manifested. Evoked and Evoker can then inter-communicate intelligibly by a mutual and mysterious thought-transmission. "The departed soul will give counsel to the operator; it will occasionally reveal secrets which may be beneficial to those

The Devil attempting to seize a magician who had formed a pact with him, is prevented by a Lay Brother.

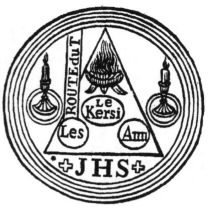

THE TRIANGLE OF THE PACTS

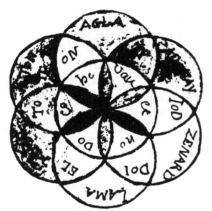

PENTACLE FOR CONJURING
INFERNAL SPIRITS

THE MAGIC CIRCLE

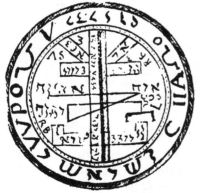

THE GREAT PENTACLE

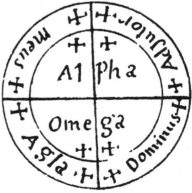

THE MAGIC CIRCLE

whom it loved on earth. In certain cases, it will however, declare itself either happy or in punishment. If it be the latter, it will ask for the prayer of the Magus, or for some religious observance, which we must unfailingly fulfill. Lastly, it will indicate the time when the evocation may be renewed.

"When it has disappeared, the operator must turn to the East, rekindle the fire on the altar, and make a final offering of incense. Then he must detach the crown and the garlands, take up his candle, and retire with his face to the West till he is out of the Oratory. His last duty is to burn the final remains of the flowers and leaves. Their ashes, united to those which have been collected during the time of retreat, must be mixed with myrtle seed and secretly buried in a field at a depth which will secure it from disturbance of the ploughshare."

The last two examples are, of course, those of "white" necromancy. The procedure followed by savage tribes of course is totally different. Among certain Australian tribes the necromants are called Birraark. It is said that a Birraark was supposed to be intitiated by the "mrarts" (ghosts) when they met him wandering in the bush. It was from the ghosts that he obtained replies to questions concerning events passing at a distance, or yet to happen, which might be of interest or moment to his tribe. An account of a spiritual seance in the bush is given in "Kamilaroi and Kurnai:" "The fires were let down; the Birraark uttered the cry "Coo-ee" at intervals. At length, a distant reply was heard, and shortly afterwards the sound as of persons jumping on the ground in succession. A voice was then heard in the gloom asking in a strange intonation 'What is wanted?" At the termination of the seance, the spirit voice said "We are going." Finally, the Birraark was found in the top of an almost inaccessible tree, apparently asleep."

"In Japan, ghosts can be raised in various ways. One mode is to "put into an andon" (a paper lantern in a frame), "a hundred rushlights, and repeat an incantation of a hundred lines. One of these rushlights is taken out at the end of each line, and the would-be ghost-seer then goes out in the dark with one light still burning, and blows it out, when the ghost ought to appear. Girls who have lost their lovers by death often try that sorcery."

The mode of procedure as practised in Scotland was thus. The haunted room was made ready. He, "who was to do the daring deed, about nightfall entered the room, bearing with him a table, a chair, a candle, a compass, a crucifix if one could be got, and a Bible. With the compass he cast a circle on the middle of the floor, large enough to hold the chair and the table. He placed within the circle the chair and the table, and on the table he laid the Bible and the crucifix besides the lighted candle. If he had not a crucifix, then he drew the figure of a cross on the floor within the circle. When all this was done, he rested himself on the chair, opened the Bible, and waited for the coming of the spirit. Exactly at midnight the spirit came. Sometimes the door opened slowly, and there glided in noiselessly a lady sheeted in white with a face of woe and told her story to the man on his asking her in the name of God what she wanted. What she wanted was done in the morning, and the spirited rested ever after. Sometimes the spirit rose from the floor and sometimes came forth from the wall. One there was who burst into the room with a strong bound, danced wildly round the circle and flourished a long whip round the man's head, but never dared to step within the circle. During a pause in his frantic dance he was asked in God's name, what he wanted. He ceased his dance and told his wishes. His wishes were carried out, and the spirit was in peace."

In Wraxalls' "Memoirs of the Courts of Berlin, Dresden, Warsaw, and Vienna" there is an amusing account of the raising of the ghost of Chevalier de Saxe. Reports had been circulated that at his palace at Dresden there was secreted a large sum of money, and it was urged that if his spirit could be compelled to appear, interesting secrets might be extorted from him. Curiosity, combined with avarice, accordingly prompted his principal heir, Prince Charles, to try the experiment, and, on the appointed night Schrepfer was the operator in raising the apparition. He commenced his proceedings by retiring into the corner of the gallery where, kneeling down with many mysterious ceremonies, he invoked the spirit to appear. At length a loud clatter was heard at all windows on the outside, resembling more the affect produced by a number of wet fingers drawn over the edge of glasses than anything else to which it could be compared.

This sound announced the arrival of the good spirits, and was shortly followed by a yell of a frightful and unusual nature, which indicated the presence of malignant spirits. Schrepfer continued his invocations, when "the door suddenly opened with violence, and something that resembled a black ball or globs rolled into the room. It was developed in smoke or cloud, in the midst of which appeared a human face, like the countenance of the Chevalier de Saxe, from which issued a loud and angry voice, exclaiming in German, "Carl, was wollte duemitmich?"—Charles, what would thou do with me?" By reiterated exorcisms Schrepfer finally dismissed the apparition, and the terrified spectators dispersed fully convinced of his magical powers.

TRANSFORMATION OF SORCERERS

CHAPTER III

ON INVOCATIONS

Spirits can communicate spontaneously, or come at our call; that is, on invocation. Some persons think we should abstain from invoking such or such a spirit, and that it is preferable to wait for the one who wishes to communicate. This opinion is founded on the fact that, in calling a designated spirit, we are not certain that it is he who presents himself, while he who comes spontaneously, and of his own impulse, better proves his identity, as he thus announces his desire to converse with us. In our opinion this is an error; firstly, because there are always spirits around us, most of them of a low class, who ask no better than to communicate; in the second place, and for this last reason alone in not calling any one in particular, the door is open to all who wish to enter. In an assembly, not to give the word to any one in particular; the door is open to all who wish to enter; and the result of this is well known. The direct appeal made to a designated spirit, is a bond between him and us; we call him by our desire, and thus erect a kind of barrier against intruders. Without a direct appeal, a spirit would often have no motive for coming to us, unless it might be our familiar spirit. These two methods have each their advantages, and the difficulty would be only in the absolute exclusion of one of the two. There is no trouble in regard to spontaneous communications where one is master of the spirits, and is certain not to let the bad gain any dominion; then it is often useful to wait the good pleasure of those who desire to communicate, because their thought is under no restraint; and in this way very admirable things may be obtained, while you cannot be sure that the spirit you call will be disposed to speak, or capable of doing so, in the sense that is desired. The scrupulous examination we have advised is guarantee against evil communications. In regular reunions, especially in those engaged on a continuous work, there are always the accustomed spirits, who are at the rendezvous without being called, because, by reason of the regularity of the seances, they are pre-engaged; they often begin spontaneously to treat a certain subject, develop a proposition, or prescribe what should be done; and then they are easily recognized, whether by the form of their language, or their writing, or by certain habits familiar to them.

When it is wished to communicate with a designated spirit, he must of necessity be invoked. If he can come, this answer is usually obtained: Yes; or, I am here; or, What do you want of me? Sometimes he enters directly into the matter, answering by anticipation the questions we proposed to address to him.

When a spirit is invoked for the first time, it is best to designate him with some precision. In the questions addressed to him, we should avoid dry, imperative forms; they might be a reason for his withdrawal. The forms should be affectionate or respectful according to the spirit, and in all cases testify the kindness of the invocator.

We are often surprised at the promptitude with which an invoked spirit presents himself, even the first time; it might be said he has been forewarned; that is, indeed, what has been done when we are thinking of making an invocation. This thinking is a kind of anticipated invocation, and as we always have our familiar spirits, who are identified with our thoughts, they prepare the way, so that nothing opposes it; the spirit whom we wish to call is already present. When this is not the case, the familiar spirit of the medium, or of the interrogator, or one of the habitues, goes to find him, which does not require much time. If the invoked spirit cannot come instantly, the messenger (the heathens would have said Mercury) asks for a delay, sometimes of five minutes, a quarter of an hour, and even several days, and when he arrives, he says he is there; and then we can begin the questions we want to ask him. The messenger is not always a necessary intermediary, for the appeal of the invocator may be heard directly by the spirit.

When we say, the invocation in the name of God, we mean that our recommendation should be taken seriously, and not lightly; those who see in it only a formula, and of little consequence, would better abstain from it. Invocations often present more difficulties to mediums than spontaneous dictation, especially when exact answers are wanted to circumstantial questions. For that end special mediums are required at once flexible and positive; and we have seen that these last are quite rare, for, as we have said, the fluidic relations (rapports) are not always instantaneously established with the first spirit comer. It is, therefore, best that mediums should not attempt special invocations, until assured of the development of their faculty, and of the nature of the spirits who assist them; for with those who are badly surrounded, the invocations could have no character of authority.

Mediums are generally much more sought for invocations of private interest then for communications of general interest; this is explained by the very natural desire we have to converse with those who are dear to us. We consider that we ought to make several important recommendations on this subject to mediums. First, to accede to this desire only with the utmost reserve with persons in whose sincerity they cannot completely trust, and to be on their guard against the snares that malicious persons might set for them. Secondly, not to lend themselves to it under any pretext, if they discover motives of curiosity or interest, and not a serious intention on the part of the invocator; to refuse themselves to all idle questions, or those aside from the circle of questions that may rationally be addressed to spirits. The suggestions should be addressed to spirits. The suggestions should be put with clearness, perspicuity, and without evasion, if categorical answers are desired.

All those that have an insidious character should be declined, for it is well known that spirits do not like those intended to put them to the proof· to insist on questions of this nature is to wish to be deceived. The, invocator should go frankly and openly to the desired end, without subterfuge or windings; if he fears to explain himself, he would better abstain. If invocations are made in the absence of the one has requested them. it should be done with the greatest prudence; it is even often times preferable to abstain entirely, those persons alone being fit to criticise the answers, to judge of the identity, to challenge explanations if there is cause, and to put incidental questions brought up by circumstances. Besides, their presence is a bond which attracts the spirit, often little disposed to communicate with strangers for whom he has no sympathy. In a word, the medium should avoid all that could transform him into a consulting agent, which, in the eyes of many persons is synonymous with a fortune-teller.

Fig. 142. THE WITCH OF ENDOR EVOKING THE PROPHET SAMUEL.

Spirits who may be invoked

All spirits, to whatever degree of the scale they belong, may be invoked—the good, as well as the bad; those who have left this life but lately, and those who have lived in the most remote times; illustrious men and the most obscure who are indifferent to us; but it is not said that they will or can always come at our call: independently of their will, or if the permission may be refused them by a superior power, they might be prevented by motives which it is not always given to penetrate.

We would say, there is no absolute hindrance to communications except what we shall presently give; the obstacles that might hinder the manifestation of a spirit are almost always individual, and pertain to circumstances.

Among the causes that might oppose the manifestation of a spirit, some are personal to him, some foreign. We must place among the former his occupations, or the missions in which he is engaged, and from which he cannot turn aside to yield to our wishes; in such case, his visit is only postponed.

There is, again, his own situation. While the state of incarnation may not be an absolute obstacle, it may be a hindrance at certain given moments, especially when it takes place in inferior worlds, and when the spirit himself is but little dematerialized. In the superior worlds, in those where the ties of spirit and matter are very feeble, the manifestation is almost as easy as in the wandering state, and in all cases easier than in those where the corporal matter is more compact.

The foreign causes pertain principally to the nature of the medium, to that if the invoker, to the sphere in which the invocation is made, and, lastly, to the end proposed. Some mediums receive more especially communications from their failiar spirits, who may be more or less elevated; others are capable of serving as intermediaries to all spirits; that depends on the sympathy or antipathy, the attraction or repulsion, which the personal spirit of the medium exercises over the foreign spirit who may take him for interpreter with pleasure or with repugnance. That, again, setting aside the innate qualities of the mediums depends on the development of the medianimic faculty. Spirits come more willingly, are more exvlicit with a medium who offers them no material obstacle. All things, besides, being equal as to moral conditions, the greater facility a medium has in writing or expressing himself the more his relations with the spirit world may be generalized.

The facility with which the habit of communicating with such or such a spirit gives, must also be taken into consideration; with time the foreign spirit identifies himself with the spirit of the medium, and with him who calls him. The question of sympathy with render communications are more prompt; this is why a first conversation is not always as satisfying as might be desired, and it also is why the spirits themselves often ask to be recalled. The spirit who is in the habit of coming in as if at home; he is familiarized with his auditors, and with his interpreters; he speaks and acts more freely.

To recapitulate: From what we have just said, it results that the power of invoking any spirit whatever does not imply that the spirit is at our orders; he can come at one moment. and not at another, which such medium or such invocator as pleases him, and not with such other; say what he pleases, without being constrained to say what he does not wish to say; go when it is agreeable to him; finally from causes dependent or not upon his will, after having shown himself assiduously during some time, he may suddenly cease to come. It is from all these motives that when we desire to call a new spirit, it is necessary to ask for our guide protector, if the invocation is possible; in cases where it may not be, he quite generally gives the motives, and then it is useless to insist.

An important question presents itself here—that of knowing whether or not there would be disagreeable consequences from invoking a bad spirit. That depends on the end proposed, and the ascendency that can be had over them. There is no difficulty when we call them with a serious and instructive aim or with a view of improving them; or commanding them, it is very great, on the contrary, if it is from pure curiosity or pleasantry or if one puts himself over their power by demanding of them any service whatever.

The good spirits, in such case, can very well give them the power to do what is asked of them, safe to punish severely afterward the rash man who dared to invoke their help and believe them more powerful than God. It is vain that he may have promised himself to make a good use of it in the end, and to dismiss the servitor once the service is rendered; the very service solicited, however minute it may be, is a veritable pact concluded with the bad spirit, and he never lets himself be used easily.

Ascendency is exercised over the inferior spirits only by moral superiority

The perverse spirits feel their masters in good men; with those who oppose to them only strength of will, a kind of brute force they struggle, and are often stronger. A person tried in this way to tame a rebellious spirit by his will; the spirit answered him, "Let me alone, with your bulling airs, you who are not better than I; they might say, a thief preaching to a thief."

One is not astonished that the name of God invoked against them should often be powerful. St. Louis has given the reason in the following manner:—The name of God has influence over imperfect spirit only in the mouth of him who can use it with authority by his virtues; in the mouth of a man who has no moral superiority over the spirit, it is a word the same as another, it is the same with the holy things opposed to the most terrible arms are inoffensive in hands unskilled in their use, or incapable of bearing them."

Language to hold with Spirits

The degree of superiority or inferiority of the spirits naturally indicates the tone it is proper to take with them. It is evident that the more elevated they are, the more right they have to our respect, to our regard, and to our submission. We should show them as much deference as we should have done during their lives, but from different motives; on the earth we should have considered their rank and their social position; in the world of spirits our respect is addressed only to moral superiority. Their very elevation raises them above the puerilies of our adulatory forms. It is not

39

EXORCISM OF A POSSESSED WOMAN

by words that we can secure their kind feeling, but by the sincerity of our sentiments. It would be ridiculous, then, to give them the titles which our usages consecrate to the distinction of ranks, and which, during their lives, might have flattered their vanity; if they are really superior, they not only will not care for them, but to do so will displease them. A good thought is more agreeable to them than the most flattering epithets; if it were other wise, they would not be above humanity. The spirit of a venerable ecclesiastle, who in this world, was a prince of the church, a good man, practicing the law of Jesus, answered once to a person who invoked him under the title of "my lord," "You should at least say, ex-my Lord, for here is no other Lord but God; know that I see who on earth knelt before me, and those before whom I myself bowed."

As to the inferior spirits, their character shows us the language proper to use with them. Among the number there are some who, though inoffensive, and even kind, are trifling, ignorant, stupid: to treat them the same as serious spirits, as some persons do is about the same as to bow before a scholar or an ass muffled in a professor's cap. A tone of familiarity would not be out of place with them, and they do not take offense at it; on the contrary, they willingly receive it.

Among the inferior spirits there are some who are unhappy. Whatever may be the faults they are expiating, their sufferings entitle them to our consideration, so much the more as no one can flatter himself that he does not deserve these words of the Christ: "Let him who is without sin among you cast the first stone." The kindness we show them is a comfort to them: in default of sympathy, they should find the indulgence we should wish them to show to us.

The spirits who reveal their inferiority by the synicism of their language, their lies, the baseness of their sentiment, the perfidy of their counsels, are assuredly less worthy of our interest than those whose words shows their repentance; we owe them, at least, the pity we accord the greatest criminals, and the way to reduce them to silence is to show ourselfves superior to them: they indulge in their perversity only among persons with whom they think there is nothing to fear; for the perverse spirits feel their masters in good men as in superior spirits.

To recapitualte: as much as it would be irreverential to treat the superior spirits as equals, just so much would it be ridiculous to extend the same deference to all without exception. Here veneration for those who deserve it, gratitude for those who protect and assist us, for all the others that kindness we may some day need for ourselves. In penetrating into the incorporeal world we learn to know it, and this knowledge should regulate us in our relations with those who inhabit it. The ancients, in their ignorance, elevated altars to them; for us, they are only creatures more or less perfect, and we raise our altars only to God.

Utility Of Special Invocations

The communications obtained from very superior spirits, or from those who have animated the great personages of antiquity, are precious from their exalted teachings. These spirits have acquired a degree of perfection which permits them to embrace a more extended sphere of ideas, to penetrate mysteries beyond the ordinary limits of humanity, and consequently, to initiate us better than others to certain things. It does not follow that communications from less elevated spirits should be without utility; the observer may draw more than one instruction. To know the manners of a people, it must be studied in every degree of the scale. He who has seen it under one aspect only, would only know it. The history of a people is not that of its kings and upper social circles; to judge it, one should see it in its private life and customs.

Now, the superior spirits are the upper circles of the spirit world: their, very elevation places them so much above us that we are frightened at the distance that separates us. Spirits more bourgeois (may they excuse the expression) make the circumstances of their new existence more palpable to us.

With them, the tie between corporeal life and spirit life is more intimate; we comprehend it better, becasue it touches us more nearly. In learning from themselves what has become of the men of all conditions and of all characters, and of all things and objects, what they think, what they experience, good, as well as vicious, the great and the small, the happy and the unhappy of the age, in a word the men who have lived among us, whom we have seen and known, with whose real life we are acquainted, whose virtues and whims we know,—we comprehend their joys and their sufferings, we are associated with them, and draw therefrom a moral instruction as much more profitable as the relations between them and us are more intimate. We put ourselves more easily in the place of him who has been our equal than of him whom we seen only through the mirage of a celestial glory.

Ordinary spirits show us the pracical application of the great and sublime truths of which the superior spirits teach us the theory. Besides, in the study of a science nothing is useless; Newton found his law of the forces of the universe in the simplest phenomena.

The invocation of ordinary spirits has, besides, the advantage of putting us on rapport with suffering spirits who can be comforted, and whose advancement may be facilitated by useful advice, so that we can be useful while, at the same time, instructing ourselves; there is egotism in seeking only one's own satisfaction in intercourse with the spirits, and he who disdains to extend a helping hand to the unhappy gives proof of pride. Of what use to obtain grand teachings from spirits of the highest order, if it does not make us inwardly better, more charitable, more benevolent for our brothers, both in the world and in the other? What would become of the diseased if the doctors refused to touch their sores?

QUESTIONS ON INVOCATIONS

1. "Can we invoke spirits without being mediums?

   "Every one can invoke spirits, and if those you call cannot manifest themselves materially, they are nevertheless near you, and listen to you.

2. "Does the spirit invoked always come at the call made to him?"
   That depends on the conditions in which he is, for there are circumstances in which he cannot do so."

3. "What causes might prevent a spirit from coming at our call?"

Firstly, his will; then his corporeal state, if he is re-incarnated; the missions with which he may be charged; and still further, permission may be refused him. There are spirits who can never communicate—those who, by their nature belong still to worlds inferior to the earth. Neither can those who are in the spheres of punishment, at least, without a sperior permission, which is granted only for the general good. That a spirit may be able to communicate, he must have attained the same degree of advancement as that of the world to which he is called; otherwise he is strange to the ideas of that world, and has no point of comparison. It is not the same with those who are sent on missions, or in expiation, to inferior worlds; they have the necessary ideas to reply."

4. "For what motives may the permission to communicate be refused to a spirit?"
It may be a trial or punishment for him, or for the one who calls him."

5. "How can spirits, dispersed in space or in different worlds, hear from all points of the universe the invocations that are made?"
They are often forewarned by the familiar spirits that surround you, who go to seek them; but here is a phenomenon difficult to explain to you, because you cannot yet understand the transmission of though among spirits. All I can tell you is, that the spirit you invoke, however distant he may be, receives, as it were, the rebound of the thought as a kind of electrical commotion, which he calls his attention to the side from whence comes the though addressed to him. It might be said he hears the thought, as on earth you hear the voice." "Is the universal fluid the vehicle of thought, as the air is that of sound." 'Yes, with this difference, that sound can be heard only within a very limited radius, while thought attains the infinite. The spirit, in splace, is like the traveler in the midst of a vast plain, who, hearing his name suddenly pronounced, directs his attention to the side on which he is called."
"We know that distances are but trifles to spirits; yet one is astonished to see them sometimes respond as

45

promptly to the call as if they had been all ready." "And so, indeed, they are sometimes. If the invocation is premeditated, the spirit is forewarned, and often finds himself there before he is called."

"Is the thought of the invocator more or less easily heard according to circumstances?"

"Without doubt; the spirit called by a sympathetic and kind sentiment is more quickly touched: it is to him the voice of a friend which he recognizes; without that it often happens that the invocation miscarries. The thought that springs from the invocation strikes the spirit if it is not well directed, it strikes in the void. It is with spirits as with men; if he who calls them is indifferent or antipathetic, they may hear, but do not often listen."

8. "Does the spirit invoked come voluntarily, or is he constrained to come?"

"He obeys the will of God, that is , the general law that rules the universe; and yet constraint is not the word; for he judges if it be useful to come, and there still is his free will. A superior spirit always comes when he is called for a useful end; he refuses to answer only in circles of persons either not serious, or treating the thing as a joke."

9. "Can the invoked spirit refuse to come at the call made on him?"

"Perfectly; or where would be his free will? Do you think the beings in the universe are at your orders? And do you consider yourselves obliged to answer all who pronounce your name? When I say he can refuse, I mean on the demand of the invocator, for an inferior spirit may be constrained to come by a superior spirit."

10. "Is there any means by which the invocation may oblige a spirit to come against his will?"

"None, if the spirit is your equal or your superior in mortality; I say in mortality, not in intelligence, because you have no authority over him: if he is your inferior, you can, if it is for his good, for then other spirits will second you."

11. "Is there any difficulty in invoking inferior spirits,

and is there any danger, in calling them of putting ourselves in their power?"

"They rule only those who allow themselves to be ruled. He who is assisted by good spirits has nothing to fear: he controls the inferior spirits; they do not control him. In isolation, mediums, especially those who are beginning, should abstain from such invocations.

12. "Is it necessary to be in any particular frame of mind for invocations?"

"The most essential of all dispositions is concentration of thought, when we desire aught of serious spirits. With faith and the desire of good, one is more powerful to invoke superior spirits. In elevating the soul by concentration of thought, at the moment of invocation, we are identified with good spirits, and attract them to us."

13. "Is faith necessary in invocations?"

"Faith in God, yes: faith will come for the rest if you desire good, and wish for instruction."

14. "Have men more power to invoke spirits when united by community of thought and intentions?"

"When all are united by charity and for good, they obtain grand things. Nothing is more injurious to the result of invocations than divergence of thought.

15. "Is making a chain by joining hands for some minutes, at the beginning of reunions of any use?"

"The chain is a material means, which does not promote union among you if it exists not in the thought: what is more useful is to be united in one common thought, each one calling to his side good spirits. You do not know all you might obtain in a serious reunion, from whence is banished every sentiment of pride and personality, and where reigns a perfect sentiment of mutual cordiality."

16. "Are invocations for fixed days and hours perferable?"

"Yes, and, if it be possible in the same place; the spirits come to it more willingly: it is the constant desire you have that aids the spirits to come and put themselves into communication with you. Spirits have their occupations, which they cannot leave at a moment's warning for your personal satisfaction. I say, in the same place but do not suppose this to be an absolute obligation, for spirits come everywhere: I mean, a place consecrated to that is preferable, because there concentration of thought is more perfect."

17. "Have certain objects, such as medallions and talismans, the property of attracting or repelling spirits, as some pretend?"
"That is a useless question, for you know very well that matter has action on spirits. Be very sure that no good spirit ever refuses such art; the value of talismans, of whatever nature they be, has existed for thousands of years."

18. "What must we think of spirits who give rendezvous in dismal places, and at undue hours?"
"These spirits amuse themselves at the expense of those who listen to them. It is always useless, and often dangerous, to yield to such suggestions: useless, because one gain absolutely nothing but to be mystified; dangerous not for the evil, the spirits might do, but on account of its influence on weak brains."

19. "Are there days and hours more propitious than others for invocations?"
"For spirits that is perfectly indifferent, though some claim certain days and hours aid to assist them to appear The most propitious moments are those in which the invocator can be the least disturbed by his accustomed occupations; when his body and mind are most calm."

20. "Is invocation an agreeable or a painful thing for spirits? Do they come voluntarily when they are called?"
"That depends on their character and the motives from which they are called. When the object is praiseworthy, and when the surrounding is sympathetic to them, it is agreeable to them, and even attractive; the spirits are always happy in the affection testified for them. There are those to whom it is a great happiness to communicate with men, and who suffer from the indifference in which they are left. But, as I have said, it depends upon their character; among spirits there are also misanthropes who do not like to be disturbed and whose answers show their ill humor, especially when they are called by indifferent people, in whom they are not at

all interested. A spirit has often no motive for coming at the call of an unknown person, who is indifferent to him, and almost always moved by curiosity; if he comes, he usually makes but short visits, unless there may be a serious and instructive end in view in the invocation."

Remark: We see people who invoke their relations only to ask them the most ordinary things of material life; for instance, one to know if he shall rent or sell his house, another to know what profit he shall have from his merchandise, the place where money is deposited, whether or not a cerain business will be advantageous. Our relations from beyond the tomb are interested in us only by reason of affection we have for them. If all our thought is limited to thinking them sorcerers, if we think of them only to ask favors of them, they cannot have any very great sympathy for us, and we should not be astonished at the little benevolence they sometimes evince, we must consider them too.

21. "Is there a difference between good and bad spirits, in regard to their readiness to come at our call?"
"There is a very great difference; bad spirits come voluntarily only inasmuch as they hope to govern and make dupes; but they experience a strong contrariety when they are forced to confess their faults, and only ask to go away again, like a pupil called up for correction. They can be constrained to come, by the superior spirits, as a punishment, and for the instruction of the incarnated. Invocation is painful for good spirits when they are called uselessly, for frivolities; then they do not come at all, or soon withdraw." "You may take it as a principle, that spirits, whatver they be, like no more than ourselves to serve as amusement for the curious. Often you have no other end, in invoking a spirit, than to see what he will tell you, or to question him on the particulars of his like, which he does not care to tell you, becaus³ he has no motive for giving you his confidence; and think you, he is going to put himself at the bar for your good pleasure? Undeceive yourselves; what he would not have done during his lifetime, he will not do as a spirit."

ABOMINATION DES SORCIERS

Est il rien qui soit plus damnable.
Au plus digne du feu d'enter,
Que cette engeance abominable
Des ministres de Lucifer:

Ils tirent de leurs noirs mysteres
L'horreur, la hayne le debat,
Et font de sanglans caracteres
Dans leur execrable Sabat:

C'est la que ces maudites ames
Se vont preparer leur tourmen,
Et qu'elles attisent les flamm
Qui bruslent eternellemen

50

Remark: Experience proves in fact, that invocation is always agreeable to spirits, when made with a serious and useful motive; the good come with pleasure to instruct us; those who suffer find comfort in the sympathy shown them, those whom we have known are satisfied with our remembrance. Frivolous spirits like to be invoked by frivolous persons, because that gives them an opporunity to amuse themselves at their expense; they are ill at ease with grave persons.

22. "In order to manifest themselves, do spirits always need to be invoked?"
"No; they very often present themselves without being called, and that proves that they come willingly."

23. "When a spirit comes of himself, can we be sure of his identity?"
"Not at all, for deceiving spirits often employ this means, the better to delude."

24. "When we invoke the spirit of a person by thought, does he come to us even when there are no manifestation by writing or otherwise?"
"Writing is a material means by which the spirit may attest his presence; but it is the thought that attracts him, and we show it by writing.

25. "When an inferior spirit manifests himself, can we oblige him to withdraw?"
"Yes; by not listening to him. But how do you expect him to withdraw when you amuse yourselves with his vileness? The inferior spirits attach themselves to those who listen to them with complacence, like the fools among you."

26. "Is invocation, made in the name of God, a guarantee against the intermeddling bad spirits?"
"The name of God is not a check for all perverse spirits, but it restrains many; by this means you always remove some, and you would remove many more, if it were made from the bottom of the heart, and not as a common formula."

27. "Could several spirits be invoked by name at the same time?"

51

"There is no difficulty in that; and if you had three or four hands to write, three or four spirits could answer you at the same time: this is what does happen when there are several mediums."

28. "When several spirits are simultaneously invoked, and there is but one medium, which one answers?"
"One answers for all, and he expresses the collective thought."

29. "In a seance, could the same spirit communicate with two mediums at the same time?"
"As easily as you have men who can dictate several letters at the same time."

Remark: We have seen a spirit answer at the same time to two mediums—to one in English, to another in French—and the answers were identical in sense; some were the literal translation of the others. Two spirits, invoked simultaneously by two mediums, might establish a conversation with each other; this mode of communication not being necessary for them, as they can read each other's thought, they sometimes do it for our instruction. If they are inferior spirits as they are still imbued with terrestrial passions and corporeal ideas, it might happen that they would dispute and apostrophize each other with big words, upbraid each other with their wrongs, and even throw pencils, baskets, planchettes, etc., at each other.

30. "Can a spirit, invoked at the same in different places, answer simultaneously to the questions addressed to him?"
"Yes, if it is an elevated spirit."
"In this case does the spirit divide himself? Or has he the gift of ubiquity?"
"The sun is one, yet he radiates all around throwing his rays afar without subdividing himself: it is the same with spirits. The spirit's thought is like a star that projects its light to a distance, and may be seen from all points of the horizon. The purer the spirit, the more his thought radiates and extends, like the light. The inferior spirits are too material; they can answer only to a single person at once, and cannot come if they are called elsewhere. A superior spirit, called at the same time

to two different points will answer both invocations, if they are equally serious and fervent; if not, he will give his preference to the more serious."

Remark: The same with a man who can, without changing his place, transmit his thought by signals seen from different points.

In a seance of the Parisian Society for Spirit Studies, when the question of ubiquity had been discussed, a spirit dictated spontaneously the following communcation: "You asked, this evening, what is the hierarchy of spirits as to ubiquity? Compare us to an aeronaut, who rises little by little in the air. When he leaves the ground, a very small circle can perceive him; as he rises, the circle enlarges for him; and when he has reached a certain height, he appears to an infinite number of persons. So with us: a bad spirit, who is still attached to the earth, remains in a very restricted circle, in the midst of persons who see him. If he grows in grace, if he becomes better, he can talk with several persons; and when he has become a superior spirit, he can radiate like the light of the sun, show himself to many persons and in many places, at the same time.

31. "Can the pure spirits be invoked—those who have ended their series of incarnations?"

"Yes, but very rarely: they communicate only with pure and sincere hearts, and not with the haughty and egotistical for you must be careful to distrust inferior spirits, who take this quality to give themselves more importance in your eyes."

32. "How is it that the spirit of the most illustrious men comes as readily and familiarly at the call of the most obscure?"

"Men judge spirits by themselves, and that is an error; after the death of the body, terrestrial rank no longer exists; there is but the distinction of goodness among them; and those who are good go wherever there is good to be done."

33. "At what length of time after death can a spirit be invoked?"

"It can be done at the very instant of death; but as, at this moment, the spirit is still in trouble, he answers but imperfectly."

Remark: The duration of the trouble being very variable, there can be no fixed time to make the invocation; yet it is rare if, at the end of eight days, the spirit has not sufficiently recovered to be able to answer; he can sometimes very well do so two or three days after death; it can, in any case, be tried with care; but one should usually wait twelve months.

34. "Is the invocation at the moment of death more painful for the spirit than if made later?"
"Sometimes; it is as if were torn from sleep before you are fully awakened. There are some, however, who are not at all disturbed by it, and even whom it helps out of their trouble."

35. "How can the spirit of a child, who has died very young, answer with knowledge, when, during his life, he had as yet no consciousness of himself?"
"The soul of a child is a spirit still enveloped in the swaddling-clothes of matter; but, disengaged from matter, he enjoys his spirit faculties, for spirits have no age; which proves that the spirit of the child has already lived. Yet, until he shall have become completely disengaged, he may preserve in his language some traces of the character of childhood."

Remark: The corporeal influence which makes itself felt on the spirit of the child, for a longer or shorter time, is sometimes remarked, in the same way, on the spirit of a person dying in a state of insanity. The spirit himself is not crazy, but we know that some spirits, for a time, believe themselves still in this world.

It is then not astonishing that the spirit of an insane person should still feel the fetters which, during life, opposed his free manifestation, until he becomes completely disengaged. This effect varies according to the cause of the insanity, for there are some maniacs who recover the lucidity of their ideas immediately after their death.

INVOCATION OF ANIMALS

36. "Can the spirit of an animal be invoked?"

"After the death of the animal, the intelligent principle that was in him is in a latent state; he is immediately utilized, by spirits charged with such cares, to animate new beings, in whom he continues the work of his elaboration. Thus, in the spirit world there are no spirits of wandering animals but only human spirits. This answers your question."

"How is it, then, that some persons have invoked animals and received answers?"

"Invoke a stone and it will answer you. There is always a crowd of spirits ready to speak for anything."

Remark: Just the same if you invoke a myth, or an allegorical personage, it will answer; that is, it will be answered for, and the spirit who would present himself would take its character and appearance. One day a person took a fancy to invoke Tartufe, and Tartufe came immediately; still more he talked of Orgon, of Elmire, of Damis and of Valire, of whom he gave news; as to himself, he counterfeited the hypocrite with as much art as if Tartufe had been a real personage. After, he said he was the spirit of an actor who had played that character.

Trifling spirits always profit by the inexperience of interrogators, but they take good care never to address those who they know are enlightened enough to discover their impostures, and who would give no credit to their stories. It is the same among men.

'A gentleman had in his garden a nest of goldfinches, in which he was much interested; one day the nest disappeared; being certain that no one about the house had been guilty of its destruction, he thought of invoking the mother of the little ones; she came, and said, in very good French, "Do not accuse any one, and be easy about my little ones; the cat overthrew the nest by jumping; you will find, under the grass, all the little ones that have not been eaten." He looked, and found it so. Must he conclude that the bird had answered him? No, assuredly; but simply that a spirit knew the history of it. This proves how much appearances should be distrusted, and how just the above reply: Invoke a stone, and it will answer you.

INVOCATION OF LIVING PERSONS

37. "Is the incarnation of the spirit an absolute obstacle
to his invocation?"
"No; but the state of the body must be such, at the
time, as to permit the spirit to disengage himself. The
incarnated spirit comes as much more easily as the world
in which he finds is of a more elevated order, because
the bodies there are less material."

38. "Can the spirit of a living person be invoked?"
"Of course, as you can invoke an incarnated spirit. The
spirit of a living person can also in his moments of
liberty, come without being invoked; that depends on
his sympathy for the person with whom he communicates."

39. "In what state is the body of the person when the spirit
is invoked?"
"He sleeps or is dozing; it is then the spirit is free."
"Could the body awaken while the spirit is absent?"
"No; the spirit is obliged to re-enter it; if, at the moment, he may be talking to you, he leaves you, and
often tells you the reason for so doing."

40. "How is the spirit, when absent from the body, warned
of the necessity of its return?"
"The spirit of a living body is never completely separated; to whatever distance it may transport itself, it
is held to the body by a fluidic bond, which serves to
recall it when necessary this tie is broken only by death."

Remark: This fluidic tie has often been noticed by seeing
mediums. It is a kind of phosphorescent train, which is lost
in space in the direction of the body. Some spirits say it is
by that they recognize those who are still bound to the
corporeal world.

41. "What would happen, if, during sleep, and in the absence of the spirit, the body should be mortally wound-
ed?"
"The spirit would be warned, and would re-enter before
death."
—"So it could not happen that the body could die in the
absence of the spirit, and that on his return he could
not re-enter it?"

"No; it would be contrary to the law regulating the union of soul and body."

—"But if the blow was struck suddenly and without premeditation?"

"The spirit would be warned before the mortal blow could be given."

Remark: The spirit of a living person interrogated on this point, answered,—"If the body could die in the absence of the spirit, it would be too convenient a method of commiting hypocritical suicides."

42. "Is the spirit of a person invoked during sleep as free to communicate as that of a dead person?"

"No; matter always influences it more or less."

Remark: A person in this state, to whom this question was addressed, answered,—

"I am always chained to the ball I drag after me."

—In this state, could the spirit be hindered from coming because of its being elsewhere?"

"Yes; the spirit might be in a place where it pleased him to remain; then he would not come at the invocation, especially if it were made by some one in whom he felt no interest."

43. "Is it absolutely impossible to invoke the spirit of a person who is awake?"

"Though difficult, it is not absolutely impossible; for if the invocation carries, it may produce sleep in the person; but the spirit can communicate, as spirit, only in those moments when its presence is not necessary to the intelligent activity of the body. "

Remark: Experience proves that invocation made during a waking state may produce sleep, or, at least, an absorption bordering on sleep; but this can take place only through a very energetic will, and when the ties of sympathy exist between the two persons; otherwise the invocation does not carry. Even in a case where the invocation causes sleep, if the moment is inopportune, the person not wishing to sleep will resist, and, if he yield, his spirit will be troubled, and answer with difficulty. It thus results that the most favorable moment for the invocation of a living person is during his natural sleep, because his spirit, being free, can as well come toward the one who calls him as to go elsewhere.

When the invocation is made with the consent of the person, and he seeks to sleep for the purpose, this very desire may retard the sleep and trouble the spirit; an unforced sleep is preferable.

44. "Has a living person, on waking, a consciousness of having been invoked?"

"No; you are yourselves invoked more often than you think. The spirit alone knows it, and may sometimes leave with him a vague impression, like a dream."

—"Who can invoke us if we are but obscure beings?"

"In other existences you may have been known either in this world or in others, and have had your relations and friends the same in this world or in others. Suppose your spirit may have animated the body of the father of another person; well, then, he invokes his father; it is your spirit who is invoked, and who answers."

45. "Would the invoked spirit of a living person answer as spirit, or with the ideas pertaining to a waking state?"

"That depends on his elevation; but his judgment is more health, and he has fewer prejudices, exactly like somnambulists; it is a nearly similar state."

46. "If the spirit of a somnambulist in a state of magnetic sleep were invoked, would he be more lucid than that of other persons?"

"He would, doubtless, answer more lucidly, because more disinthralled; all depends on the degree of the spirits independence of the body."

—"Could the spirit of a somnambulist answer a person at a distance, who might invoke him, at the same time that he is verbally answering another persons?"

"The faculty of communicating simultaneously at two different points pertains only to spirits completely disengaged from matter."

47. "Can the ideas of a person in a waking state be modified by acting upon his spirit during sleep?"

"Yes, sometimes; the ties that binds the spirit to matter are not then so close; he is more accessible to moral impressions, and these impressions may influence his mode of seeing in the ordinary state."

48. "Is the spirit of a living person free to say or not to say what he will?"
"He has his faculties of spirit and consequently his free will; and as he has more perspicacity, he is even more circumspect than when a waking state."

49. "In invoking a person, can he be constrained to speak when he wishes to be silent?"
"I have said that the spirit has his free will; but it can very well be that, as spirit, he attaches less importance to certain things than in the ordinary state; his conscience may speak more freely. Besides if he does not wish to speak, he can easily escape importunities by leaving, for a spirit cannot be retained as you can retain his body."

50. "Can the spirit of a living person be forced by another spirit to come and speak, as can be done among wandering spirits?"
"Among spirits, whether of the dead or the living, there is no supremacy, save from moral superiority; and you may well believe that a superior spirit, will never land his support to a cowardly indiscretion.

Remark: This abuse of confidence would, in fact, be a bad action, which, however, would have no result, since you cannot tear from a spirit a secret he desires to keep, at least unless, influenced by a sentiment of justice, he avows that, under other circumstances, he would withhold. A person, by this means, desired to know of one of his relatives if his will was in her favor.

The spirit answered, "Yes, my dear niece, and you shall soon have the proof of it."

The thing was true; but a few days afterward the relative destroyed his will, and was mischievous enough to let her know of it, though he did not know he had been invoked.

An instinctive feeling, doubtless, urged him to execute the resolution his spirit had taken at the time of his having been questioned. It is cowardly to ask of a spirit, either of the dead or living, what you would not have dared to ask him in person, and this cowardice is not even compensated by the expected result.

51. "Can one invoke a spirit whose body is still in the mother's womb?"
"No; you know that, at such time, the spirit is in utter trouble."

Remark: The incarnation takes place actually only at the moment of the child" first breath; but from the conception of the spirit designated to animate it is seized with a trouble, which increases as the birth approaches and takes from him his self-consciousness, and conequently the faculty of anwering.

52. "Could a deceiving spirit take the place of a living invoked person?"
"That is not doubtful, and it very often happens, particularly when the intention of the invocator is not pure. But the invocation of living persons is interesting only as a psychological study: it is necessary to abstain always when it can have no instructive result."

Remark: If the invocation of wandering spirits does not always carry,—to use their own expression,—it must be much more frequent for those who are incarnated; then, especially, do deceiving spirits take their place.

53. "Are there dangers in the invocation of a living person?"
"It is not always without danger; that depends on the person's position for if he is sick, it might add to his sufferings."

54. "In what case could the invocation of a living person have most dangers?"
You should abstain from invoking children of a very tender age, persons seriously ill, infirm old men; indeed, there are dangers in all cases when the body is very much enfeebled."

Remark: The sudden suspension of the intellectual faculties during a waking state might also be dangerous, if the person at the moment should find himself in need of his presence of mind.

55. "During the invocation of a living person. does the body experience fatigue by reason of the work his absent spirit performs?"
"A person in this state, who said his body was fatigued, answered this question:

"My spirit is like a balloon tied to a post; my body is the post, which is shaken by the strugglings of the balloon."

56. "As the invocation of living persons may be dangerous when made without caution, does not the danger exist when we invoke a spirit we do not know to be incarnated, and who might not find himself in favorable conditions?"

"No; the circumstances are not the same since he will come only if in a position to do so; and besides, have I not told you to ask, before making an invocation, if it be possible.

57. "When, at the most inopportune moments, we experience an irresistible desire to sleep, does it warn us that we are invoked by some one?"

"It may occur, but most often it is a purely physical effect; either the body or the spirit has need of its liberty."

Remark: A lady of our acquaintance, a medium, one day invoked the spirit of her grandson, who was sleeping in the same room. His identity was confirmed by the language, by the familiar expressions of the child, and by the exact recital of several things that had happened at his boarding-school; but one especial circumstance confirmed it. Suddenly the hand of the medium paused in the middle of a sentence, and it was impossible to obtain anything further: at this moment, the child, half awake, moved in his bed. Some moments after, he again slept; the hand went on anew, continuing the interrupted talk.

The invocation of living persons, made under good conditions, proves, in the least contestable manner, the distinct action of the spirit and the body, and consequently, the existence of an intelligent principle independent of matter.

HUMAN TELEGRAPHY

58. "Could two persons, by invoking each other, transmit their thoughts, and thus correspond?"

—"Yes; and this human telegraphy will some day be a universal means of correspondence."

"Why should it not be practiced at present?"

"So it is, with some persons, but not with every one; men must purify themselves, in order that their spirit may be disengaged from matter: and this is still another reason for making the invocation in the name of God. Until then it is confined to chosen and dematerialized souls, who are rarely met in the actual state of the world's inhabitants."

CHAPTER IV

OF THE CONSECRATION OF ALL MAGICAL INSTRUMENTS AND MATERIALS WHICH ARE USED IN THIS ART

The virtues of consecrations chiefly consist in two things, viz., the power of the person consecrating, and the virtue of the prayer by which the consecration is made.

For in the person consecrating, there is required firmness, constancy, and holiness of life; and that the consecrator himself shall, with a firm and undubitable faith, believe the virtue, power, and effect thereof.

Then in the prayer by which the consecration is made it derives its virtue either from divine inspiration, or else by composing it from sundry places in the Holy Scripture, in the commemoration of some of the wonderful miracles of God, effects, promises, sacraments and sacramental things of which I have abundance in holy writ.

There must likewise be used the invocation of divine names, that are significative of the work in hand; I likewise a sanctifying and *expiation which is wrought by sprinkling with holy water, unctions with holy oil, and odoriferous suffumigations. Therefore in ever consecration there is always used a benediction and consecration of water, earth, oil, fire, and suffumigations, etc., with consecrated wax-lights or lamps burning; for without lights no consecration is duly performed. You must therefore particularly observe this, that when anything (which I call prophane) is to be used, in which there is defilement or pollution, it must, first of all, be purified by an Exorcism, composed solely for that purpose, which out to precede the consecration which things being so made pure are most apt to receive the influences of the divine virtue. You must also observe that at the end of any consecration, after the prayer is rightly performed, as I have mentioned, the operator ought to bless the thing consecrated, by breathing out some sentence with divine virtue and power of present consecration with a commemoration of his virtue and authority, that so it may be the more duly performed, and with an earnest and attentive mind. Now I shall give ye here some examples, that, by these, a path may be made to the whole perfection thereof.

THE CONSECRATION OF WATER

So in the consecration of water, you must commemorate that God has placed the firmament in the midst of the waters, and likewise that God has placed the fountain of waters in the earthly paradise, from whence sprang four holy rivers that water the whole earth; likewise we are to remember that God caused the waters to be an instrument of his justice in destroying the giants, by bringing on the deluge which covered the face of the whole earth; and in the overthrow of the host of Pharaon in the Red Sea, and that God led the children of Israel through on dry land, and through the midst of the river Jordan, and likewise his marvellously drawing water out of the stony rock in the wilderness; and that at the prayer of Samson, he caused water to flow out of the jaw-bone of an ass; and likewise that God has made water the instrument of his mercy and salvation for the expiation of original sin; also that Christ was baptized in the river Jordan, and hath thereby sanctified and cleansed the waters; likewise certain divine names are to be invocated which are conformable hereto; as, that God is a living fountain, living water, the fountain of mercy, and names of the like sort.

CONSECRATION OF FIRE

And likewise, in the consecration of fire, you are to commemorate that God hath created the fire to be an instrument to execute his justice, for punishment, vengeance, and the expiation of sins; also, when God comes to judge the world that he will command a conflagaration of fire to go before him; likewise we are to mention that God appeared to Moses in a burning bush; and also how he went before the children of Israel in a pillar of fire; that nothing can be duly offered, sanctified or sacrificed without fire; and how that god instituted fire to be kept in continually in the tabernacle of the convenant; and how miraculously he rekindled the same, being extinct, and preserved it elsewhere from going out being hidden under the waters; and things of this sort; likewise the names of God are to be called upon which are consonant to this; as you read in the law and prophets, that God is a consuming fire; and likewise if there are any divine names which signify fire, as the glory of

God, the light of God, the splendor and brightness of God, &c.

THE CONSECRATION OF OIL

And likewise in the consecration of oil and perfumes you are to mention such things as are consonant to this purpose, as of the holy anoiting oil mentioned in Exodus, and divine names significant thereunto; such as is the name of Christ, which signifies anointed; and whatever mysteries there are relative to oil in the Scriptures, as the two olive-trees distilling holy oil into the lamps that burn before the face of God, mentioned in Revelations.

OF THE BENEDICTION OF LIGHTS, LAMPS, WAX, &C.

Now, the blessing of the lights, lamps, wax, &c., is taken from the fire and whatever contains the substance of the flame, and whatever similtudes are in the mysteries, as the seven candlesticks which burn before the face of God.

Therefore I have here given the manner of composing the consecrations, which first of all are necessary to be used in every kind of ceremony, and ought to precede every experiment or work, and without which nothing in magic rites can be performed duly.

In the next place, I will show thee the consecration of places, instruments, and the like things.

THE CONSECRATION PLACES, GROUND, CIRCLE, &C.

Therefore when you would consecrate any place or circle, you should take the prayer of Lamas used in the dedication and consecration of the Temple; you must likewise bless the place by sprinkling with holy water and with suffumigations, and commemorate in the benediction holy mysteries; such as these, the sanctification of thorne of God, of Mount Sinai, of the tabernacle of the covenant, of the holy of holies, of the temple of Jerusalem: also the sanctification of Mount Gologotha, by the transfiguration and ascension of Christ, &c. And by invocating all divine names which are significant to this; such as the place of

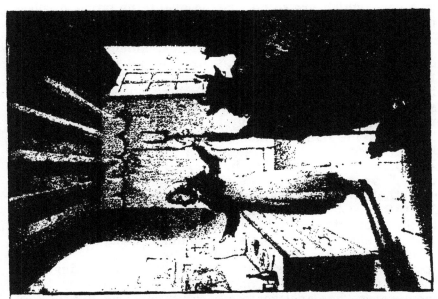

God, the chair of God, the tabernacle of God, the altar of God, the habitation of God, and the like divine names of this sort, which are to be written about the circle, or place to be consecrated.

And, in the consecration of instruments, and every other thing that is used in this Art, you must proceed after the same manner, by sprinkling with holy water the same, by fumigation, by anointing with holy oil, sealing it with some holy seal, and blessing it with prayer, and by commemorating holy things out of the sacred Scriptures, collecting divine names which are agreeable to the things to be consecrated; as for example, in the consecration of the sword we are to remember in the gospel, "he that hath two coats," &c. and that in the second of the Maccabees, it is said that a sword was divinely and miraculously sent to JUDAS MACCABEUS; and if there is anything of the like in the prophets, as "take unto you two-edged swords," &c. And you shall also, in the same manner, consecrate experiments and books, and whatever of the like nature, as writings, pictures, &c, by sprinkling, perfuming, anointing, sealing, blessing, with holy commeforations, and calling to remembrance the sanctification of mysteries; as the table of the ten commandments which were delivered to Moses by God in Mount Sinai, the sanctification of the Old and New Testaments, and likewise of the law, prophets, and Scriptures, which were promulgated by the Holy Ghost and again there are to be mentioned such divine names as are convenient to this; as these are, viz. the testament of God, the book of God, the Book of Life, the knowledge of God, the wisdom of God, and the like. And with such kind of rites as these is the personal consecration performed.

There are besides these another rite of consecration of great power and efficacy; and this is one of the kinds of superstitions, viz. when the writ of consecration or collection of any sacrament in the church is transferred to that thing which we would consecrate.

It must be noted that vows, oblations, and sacrifices, have the power of consecration also, as well real as personal; and they are as it were, certain conventions between those names with which they are made and us who make them, strongly cleaving to our desire and wished effects, as when we sacrifice with certain names, or thing; as fumigations, unctions, rings, images, mirrors; and some things less material, as characters, seals, pentacles, enchantments, orations, pictures, Scriptures, of which we have largely spoken before.

OF THE INVOCATION OF EVIL SPIRITS, AND THE BINDING OF, AND CONSTRAINING OF THEM TO APPEAR

Now if thou art desirous of binding any spirit to a ready obedience to thee, I will show you how a certain book may be made by which they may be invoked; and this book is to be consecrated a book of Evil Spirits, ceremoniously to be composed in the name and order, whereunto they bind with a certain holy oath, the ready and present obedience of the spirit. This book is therefore to be made of the most pure and clean paper, which is generally called virgin paper; and this book must be inscribed after this manner, viz. let there be drawn on the left side of the biok the image of the spirit, and on the right side thereof his character, with the oath above it, containing the name of the spirit, his dignity and place, with his office and power. Yet many magicians do compose this book otherwise, omitting the characters and images; but I think that it is much more efficacious not to neglect anything above mentioned in the forms.

There is likewise to be observed the circumstances of places, times, hours, according to the stars which these spirits are under and are seen to agree to; with their site, rite, and order, being applied.

Which book being so written, is to be well bound, adorned, garnished, embellished, and kept secure, with registers and seals lest it should happen after the consecration to open in some part not designed, and endanger the operator. And above all, let this book be kept as pure and reverent as possible; for irreverance of mind causes it to lose its virtue by pollution and phophanation.

Now this sacred book being thus composed according to the form and manner I have delivered, you are to consecrate it after a two-fold way; the first is, that all and singularly each of the spirits who are written in the book be called to the circle, according to the rites magical, which we have before taught, and place the book which is to be consecrated in a triangle on the outside of the circle; then read, in the presence of the spirits, all the oaths which are contained and written in that book; then the book to be consecrated being already placed without the circle in a triangle there drawn, compel all the spirits to impose their hands where their images and characters are drawn, and to confirm and consecrate the same with a special and common oath. This being done, let the book be shut and preserved as I have spoken before; then license the spirits to depart according to due rite and Magical order.

There is another method extant among us to consecrating a general book of spirits which is more easy, and of as much efficacy to produce every effect, except that in opening this book, the spirits do not always appear visible. And this way is thus: let be made a book of spirits, as we have before shown, but in the end thereof write invocations, bonds, and strong conjurations, wherewith every spirit may be bound; then bind this book between two lamens or tables, and on the inside thereof draw or let be drawn two Holy pentacles of the Divine Majesty, which I have before set forth, out of the Apocalypse. Then let the first of them be placed in the beginning of the book, and the second at the end of the same.

This book being thus perfected, let it be brought, in a clear and fair night, to a circle prepared in a cross-way, according to the art which I have before delivered; and there, in the first place, the book is to be opened, and to be consecrated according to the rites and ways which we have before delivered concerning consecration, which being done, let all the spirits be called which are written in the book, in their own order and place, conjuring thrice by the bonds described in the book that they come to that place within the space of three days, to assure their obedience and confirm the same, to the book so to be consecrated; then let the book be wrapped up in a clean line cloth, and bury it in the midst of the circle, and stop the hole so as it may not be perceived or discovered: the circle being destroyed after you have licensed the spirits, depart before sun-rise; and on the third day, about the middle of the night, return and make the circle anew and on thy knees make prayer unto God, and give thanks to him; and let a precious perfume be made, open the hole in which you buried your book and take it out, and so let it be kept, not opening the same. Then after licensing the spirits in their order and destroying the circle, depart before sun-rise. And this is the last rite and manner of consecrating profitable to whatever writings, experiments, &c. that direct the spirits, placing the same between the two holy Lamens or Pentacles, as is before mentioned.

But when the operator would work by the Book thus consecrated he should do it in a fair and clear season, when the spirits are least troubled; and let him turn himself towards the region of the spirits; then let him open the book under a due register, and likewise invoke the spirits by their oaths there described and confirmed, and by the name of their character and image, to whatever purpose you desire, and if there be need conjure them by the bonds placed in the end of the book. And having attained thy desired effect license them to depart.

And now I proceed to speak of the invocation of good as well as bad spirits.

The good spirits may be invocated of you, or by you, diverse ways, and they in sundry shapes and manners offer themselves to us, for they openly speak to those that watch, and do offer themselves to our sight, or do inform us by dreams and by oracle of those things which we have a great desire to know. Whoever therefore would call any good spirit to speak or appear in sight, he must particularly observe two things; one whereof is about the disposition of the invocant, the other concerning those things which are outwardly to be adhibited to the invocation for the conformity of the spirit to be called.

It is necessary therefore that the invocant religiously dispose himself for the space of many days to such a mystery, and to conserve himself during the time chaste, abstinent, and to abstract himself as much as he can from all manner of foreign and secular business; I likewise he should observe fasting, as much as shall seem convenient to him, and let him daily between sunrising and setting, being clothed in pure white line, seven times call upon God, and make a deprecation to the angels to be called and invocated, according to the rule which I have before taught. Now the number of days of fasting and prepartion is commonly one month, i. e. the time of a whole lunation. Now, in the Hindue Cabala, we generally prepare ourselves forty days before.

Now concerning the place, it must be chosen clean, pure, close, quiet, free from all manner of noise, and not subject to any stranger's sight. This place must first of all be exorcised and consecrated; and let there, be a table or altar placed therein covered with a clean white linen cloth and set towards the east. In the middle of the altar let there be placed lamens, or the holy paper I have before described, covered with fine linen, which is not to be opened until the end of the days of consecration. You shall also have in readiness a precious perfume and a pure anointing oil.—And let them both be kept consecrated. Then set a censor on the head of the altar, wherein you shall kindle the holy fire and make a precious perfume every day that you pray.

Now for your habit, you shall have a long garment of white linen, close before and behind, which may come down over the feet, and gird yourself about the loins with a girdle. You shall likewise have a veil made of pure white linen on which must be wrote in a gilt lamen, the name Rajpore-Kogur; all things which are to be consecrated and sanctified in order. But you must not go into this holy place till it be first washed and covered with a cloth new and clean, and then you may enter, but with your feet naked and bare; and when you enter therein you shall sprinkle with holy water, then make a perfume upon the altar; and then on thy knees pray before the altar as we have directed.

Now when the time is expired, on the last day, you shall fast more strictly; and fasting on the day following, at the rising of the sun, enter the holy place, using the ceremonies before spoken of, first by sprinkling thyself, then making a perfume, you shall sign the cross with holy oil in the forehead, and anoint your eyes, using prayer in all these consecrations. Then, open the lamen and pray before the altar upon your knees; and then an invocation may be made as follows:

AN INVOCATION OF THE GOOD SPIRITS

In the name of the Most Eminent Adepts, I do desire thee, strong and mighty spirits (here name the spirits you would have appear) that if it be the divine will of him who is called Rajpore-Kogur, the holy adept, the Powerful, that thou take upon thee some shape as best becometh thy celestial nature and appear to me visably here in this place, and answer my demands, in as far as I shall not transgress the bonds of the divine mercy and goodness, by requesting unlawful knowledge; but that thou wilt graciously show me what things are most profitable for me to know and do to the glory and honour of his divine Majesty who liveth and reigneth, world without end. Amen.

Lord thy will be done on earth as it is in heaven— make clean my heart within me, and take not thy holy spirit from me. O Lord, by thy name I have called them, suffer the to administer unto me.

And that all things may work together for thy honour and glory, to whom with thee, the Son and blessed Spirit, be ascribed all might, majesty, and dominion world without end. Amen.

The invocation being made, the good spirits will appear unto you which you desire, which you shall entertain with a chaste communication, and license them to depart.

Now the Lamen which is used to invoke any good spirit must be made after the following manner: either in metal comformable or in new wax mixed with convenient spices and colours; or it may be made with pure white paper with convenient colours, and outward form of it may be either square, circular, or triangular, or of the like sort according to the rule of the numbers, in which there must be written the divine names, as well general as special. And in the centre of the lamen draw a nexagon or character of six corners, in the middle thereof write the name and character of the star, or of the spirit his governor, to whom the good spirit that is to be called is subject. And about this character let there be placed so many characters of five corners or pentacles as the spirits we would call together at once. But if you shall call only one, nevertheless there must be made four pentagons, wherein the name of the spirit or spirits, with their characters, are to be written. Now this lamen must be composed when the moon is in her increase on those days and hours which agree to the spirit; and if you take a fortunate planet therewith, it will be better for producing the effect: which table or lamen being rightly made in the manner I have fully described, must be conse-created according to the rules above delivered.

I will yet declare unto you another rite more easy to perform this thing: let the disciple who wishes to receive an oracle from a spirit be chaste, pure and sanctified; then a place being chose pure, clean, and covered with clean and white linen, everywhere, on the Lord's day in the new of the moon, let him enter into the place clothed with white linen; let him exorcise the place, bless it, and make a circle there with a consecrated coal; let there be written in the outer part of the circle the names of the angels; in the inner part thereof write the mighty names of God; and let be placed within the circle, at the four parts of the world, the vessels for the perfumes. Then, being washed fasting, let him enter the place and pray towards the east this whole Psalm "Blessed are the undefiled in the way,"&c. Psalm cxix. Then make a fumigation, and deprecate the spirits by the said divine names, that they will appear unto you, and reveal or discover that which you so earnestly desire; and do this continually for six days, washed and fasting. On the seventh day, being washed and fasting, enter the circle, perfume it and anoint thyself with holy oil upon the forehead, eyes, and in the palms of both hands, and upon the feet; then, with bended knees say the Psalm aforesaid, with divine and angelical names. Which being said, arise, and walk round the circle from East to West, until thou shalt be wearied with a giddiness of the head and brain, then straitway fall down in the circle, where thou mayest rest, and thou wilt be wrapped up in an ectasy; and a spirit will appear and inform thee of all things necessary to be known. We must observe also, that in the circle there ought to be four holy candles burning at the four parts of the world, which ought not to want light for the space of a week.

The Prince
of Darkness.

THE MAGIC CIRCLE

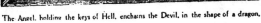

The Angel, holding the keys of Hell, enchains the Devil, in the shape of a dragon.

THE HAND OF GLORY

And the manner of fasting is this: to abstain from all things having a life of sense, and from those which do proceed from them, let him drink only pure running water; neither is there any food or wine to be taken till the going down of the sun.

Let the perfume and the holy anointing oil be made as is set forth in Exodus, and other holy books of the Bible. It is also to be observed, that as often as he enters the circle he has upon his forehead a golden lamen, upon which there must be written the name Rajpore-Kogur, in the manner I have before mentioned.

OF ORACLES BY DREAMS

But natural things and their own mixtures do likewise belong unto my disciples, and I always use such to receive oracles from a spirit by a dream; which are either by perfumes, unctions, meats, candles, seals, rings, etc.

Now those who are desirous to receive oracles in or through a dream, let him make himself a ring of the sun or Saturn for this purpose. There are likewise images of dreams, which being put under the head when he goes to sleep, doth effectually give true dreams of whatever the mind hath before determined or consulted upon, the practice of which is as follows:

Thou shalt make an image of the sun, the figure whereof must be a man sleeping upon the bosom of an angel, which thou shalt make when Leo ascends, the sun being in the ninth house in Aries: thou shalt write upon the figure the name of the effect desired, and in the hand of the angel the name of the intelligence of the sun. Let the same image be made in Virgo ascending, Mercury being fortunate in Aries in the ninth; or Gemini ascending, Mercury being fortunate in the ninth house in Aquarius; and let it be received with Saturn with a fortunate aspect, and let the name of the spirit be written upon it. Let the same likewise be made in Libra ascending, Venus being received from Mercury in Gemini in the ninth house, and write upon it the angel of Venus. Again, you may make the same image Aquarius ascending, Saturn fortunately possessing the ninth in his exaltation. which is Libra; and let there be written upon it the angel of Saturn. The same may be made Cancer ascending, the moon being received by Jupiter and Venus in Pisces, and being fortunately placed in the ninth house, and write upon it the spirit of the moon.

There are likewise made rings of dreams of wonderful efficacy; and there are rings of the sun and Saturn; and the constellation of them is when the sun or Saturn ascend in their exaltations in the ninth, and when the moon is joined to Saturn in the ninth, and in that sign which was the ninth house of the nativity; and write and engrave upon the rings the name of the spirits of the sun or Saturn; and by these rules you may know how and by what means to constitute more of thyself: but know this, that such images, work nothing (as they are simple images) unless they are vividfied by a spiritual and celestial virtue, and chiefly by the ardent desire and firm intent of the soul of the operator. But who can give a soul to an image, or make a stone, or metal, or clay, or wood, or wax, or paper to live? Certainly no man; he only hath it who transcends the progress of angels, and comes to the very architype himself.

The tables of numbers likewise confer to the receiving of oracles, being duly formed under their own constellations. Holy tables and papers likewise serve to this effect, being especially composed and consecrated; such as the Almutel of Solomon, and the Table of the Revolution of the name of Tetragrammaton; and those things which are of this kind, and written to produce grammaton, and those things which are of this kind, and written to produce these effects, out of various figures, numbers, holy Scriptures, and pictures, with inscriptions of holy angels; the composition whereof is taken out of diverse places of the holy Scriptures, Psalms, and versicles, and other certain promises out of the divine revelations and prophecies.

To the same effect do conduce, likewise, holy prayers and deprecations as well to God as to the blessed angels; the deprecations of which prayers are to be composed as we have before shown, according to some religious similiture, making mention of those things which we intend to do; as out of the Old Testament of the dream of Jacob, Joseph, Pharoah, Daniel and Nebuchadnezzar: if out of the New Testament, of the dream of Joseph; of the three wise men, or Magi, of John the evangelist sleeping upon the breast of our Lord; and whatever of the like kind can be found in religion, miracles, and revelation. According to which the deprecation may be composed; if when he goes to sleep it be with a firm intention, and then, without doubt, they will afford a wonderful affect.

Therefore he who is desirous of receiving true oracles by dreams, let him abstain from supper, from drink, and be otherwise well disposed, so his brain will be free from turbulent vapours; let him also have his bed-chamber fair and clean: exorcised and consecrated if he will; then, let him perfume the same with some convenient fumigation, and let him anoint his temples with some unguent efficacious hereunto, and put a ring of dreams upon his finger; then let him take one of the images we have spoken of, or some holy table, or prayer, and place the same under his head; then, having made a devout prayer, let him address himself to sleep, meditating upon that thing which he desires to know; so shall he receive a most certain and undoubted oracle by a dream, when the moon goes through that sign which was in the ninth house of his nativity, and also when she goes through the sign of the ninth of the revolution of his nativity, and when she is in the ninth sign from the sign of perfection.

This is the way whereby we obtain all sciences and Arts whatsoever, whether Alchemy, Magic, or else, suddenly and perfectly with a true illumination of our intellect; although all inferior familiar spirits whatsoever conduce to this effect, and sometimes also evil spirits sensibly inform us intrinsically and extrinsically.

OF THE METHOD OF RAISING EVIL OR FAMILIAR SPIRITS BY A CIRCLE; LIKEWISE THE SOULS AND ASTRAL BODIES OF THE DEAD

It is here convenient that I say something about the means used by the Hindus to raise up what are usually termed evil spirits to the circle, and the methods of calling up the Astral of souls of those who have died a violent or premature death.

Now if ye would call any evil spirit to the circle, ye must first consider and know his nature, and to which of the planets it agrees, and what offices are distributed unto him from the planet. This being known, let there be sought out a place fit and convenient, and proper for his invocation, according to the nature of the planet and the quality of the offices of the same spirit, as near as it can be done; as if their power be over the sea, rivers, or floods, then let the place be the sea-shore, and so of the rest. Then chose a convenient time both for the quality of the air (being serene, quiet, clear and fitting for the spirits to assume bodies) ; as also of the quality of and nature of the planet and the spirit, as on his day and time in which he rules; he may be fortunate or unfortunate sometimes of the day, and sometimes of the night, as the stars and spirits do require.

These things being judiciously considered, let the circle be made at the place elected, as well for the deference of the invocant as the confirmation of the spirit. And in the circle write the divine general names, and all those things which do yield deference to us; and, with them, those divine names which do rule his planet, and the offices of the spirit himself; likewise write therein the names of the good spirits which bear rule in the time you do this, and are able to bind and constrain that spirit which you intend to call. And if ye will further strengthen and fortify your circle, you may add characters and pentacles agreeing to the work; then also, if ye will, you may either, within or without the circle frame an angular figure with the inscription of such convenient numbers as are congruent amongst themselves to my work, which are to be known according to the manner of numbers and figures delivered in my first book.

Further you are to be provided with lights, perfumes, unguents, and medicines, compounded according to the nature of the spirit and planet which agree with the spirit by reason of their natural and celestial virtue.

Then you are to be furnished with holy and consecrated things necessary, not only for the defence of the invocant and his companions, but also serving for bonds to bind and constrain the spirits; such as holy papers, lamens, pictures, pentacles, swords, scepters, garments of convenient colour and matter.

Then, with all these things provided, let the exorcist and his companions go into the circle. In the first place, let him consecrate the circle and every thing he uses; which being done in a solemn and firm manner, with convenient gesture and courtenance, let him begin to pray with a loud voice after the manner following. First, by making an oration or prayer to God, and then entreating the good spirits; but you should read some prayer, or psalm, or gospel, for our defence in the first place. After those prayers and orations are said, let him begin to invocate the spirit which he desireth, with a gentle and loving enchantment to all the coasts of the world, with a commemoration of his own authority and power. Then rest and look round to see if any spirit does appear; which if he delays, then let him repeat his invocation, as above said, until he hath done it three times; and if the spirit is obstinate and will not appear, then let the invocator begin to conjure him with divine power; but so that all his conjurations and commemorations do agree with the nature and office of the spirit, and reiterate the same three times, from stronger to stronger, using contumelies, cursings, punishments, suspension from his power and office, and the like.

And after these coures are finished, cease; and if the spirit shall appear let the invocant turn himself towards the spirit, and courteously receive him, and, earnestly entreating him, let him ask in his name, which write down on your holy paper, and then proceed by asking him whatsoever you will; and if in any thing the spirit shall appear to be obstinate, ambiguous or lying, let him be bound by convenient conjurations; and if you doubt any thing, make, without the circle with the consecrated sword, the figure of a triangle or pentagon, and compel the spirit to enter into it; and if you receive any promise which you would have confirmed with an oath, stretch the sword out of the circle, and swear the spirit by laying his hand on the sword. Then having obtained of the spirit that which you desire, or are otherwise contented, license, him to depart with courteous words, giving command that he do no hurt; and if he will not depart, compel him by powerful conjurations; and if need require, expel him by exorcisms and by making contrary suffumigations; and when he is departed go not out of the circle, but make a stay, and use some prayer giving thanks to God and the good angels; and also praying for your future defence and conservation, which being orderly performed you may depart.

But if your hopes are frustrated, and no spirit will appear, yet for this you need not despair; but leaving the circle after licensing to depart (which must never be omitted whether a spirit appears or not*) return at other times, doing as before. And if you think that you have erred in anything, then you shall amend by adding or diminishing; for the constancy or repetition increases your authority and power, and strikes a terror into the spirits, and compels them to obey.

And often the spirits do come although they appear not visible (to cause terror to him who calls them,) either in the thing which he uses, or else in the operation itself. But this kind of licensing is not given simply, but by a kind of dispensation, with suspension, until they shall render themselves obedient; also, without a circle, these spirits may be called to appear, by the way we have delivered in the consecration of a book. But when we intend to execute any effect where an apparition is not needful, then that is to be done, by making and forming that which is to be done, by making and forming that which is to be to us an instrument; as whether it be an image, ring, character, table, writing, candle, sacrifice, or any thing else; then the name of the spirit is to be written therein with his character, according to the exigency of the experiment, either by writing it with blood, or otherwise using a perfume agreeable to the spirit. Likewise we are often to make orations and prayers to God and the good angels before we invocate any evil spirit, conjuring him by divine power.

(*They who neglect licensing the spirits are in very great danger, because instance have been known of the operator experiencing a sudden shock.)

I will now inform thee farther, that those souls do still love their relinquished bodies after death, a certain affinity alluring them as it were. Such are the souls of noxious men who have violently relinquished their bodies and souls wanting a due burial, which still wander in a liquid and turbulent spirit above their dead carcasses; but these souls, by the known means by which they were joined to their bodies, by the like vapours, liquors, and savours, are easily drawn into them.

Hence it is that the souls of the dead are not to be called up without blood or by the application of some part of their relict body.

In the raising therefore of these Astral Spirits, you are to perfume with new blood the bones of the dead, and with flesh, eggs, milk, honey, and oil, which furnish the soul with a medium apt to receive its body.

It is likewise to be understood, those who are desirous to raise any souls of the dead, ought to select those places wherein these kind of souls are most known to be conversant; or by some alliance alluring the souls into their forsaken bodies, or by the forcible nature of some place fitted and prepared to purge or punish these souls; which places for the most part, are to known by the appearance of visions, nightly incursions and apparitions.

Therefore the places most fitting for these things are church-yards. And better than them are those places devoted to the executions of criminal judgments; and better than these are those places where, of late years, there have been so great and so many public slaughters of men; and that place, is still better than those where some dead carcass that came by violent death is not yet expiated, not was lately buried; for the expiation of those places is likewise a holy rite duly to be adhibited to the burial of the bodies, and often prohibits the soul returning to its body, and expels the same afar off to the place of judgment.

And from hence it is that the souls of the dead are not easy to be raised up, except it be the souls of them whom we know to be evil, or to have perished by a violent death, and whose bodies do want the rite of due burial.

Now although I have spoken concerning such places of this kind, it will not be safe or commodious to go unto them; but it is requisite for you to take to whatsoever place is to be chosen some principal relict of the body, and therewith make a perfume in due manner, and to perform other competent rites.

It is also be known, that because the souls are certain spiritual lights, therefore artificial lights framed out of certain competent things compounded according to a true rule, with congruent inscriptions of names and seals, do very much avail to the raising up of departed souls. But those things which are now spoken of are not always sufficient to raise up souls, because of an extra-natural portion of understanding and reason, which is above and known only to the heavenly destinies and their powers.

You should therefore allure the said souls by supernatural and celestial powers duly administered, even by those things which do move the very harmony of the soul as well imaginative as rational and intellectual, such as voices, songs, sounds, enchantments; and religious things, as prayer conjurations, exorcisms, and other holy rites, which may commodiously be administered hereunto.

The following instructions are the principal and sum total of all I have said, only I have brought it rather into a closer train of experiment and practice than any of the rest; for here you may behold the distinct functions of the spirits; likewise the whole perfection of Magical Ceremonies is here described, syllable by syllable.

But as the greatest power is attributed to the circles; (for they are certain fortresses,) I will now clearly explain, and show the composition and figure of a circle.

THE COMPOSITION OF A CIRCLE

The forms of circles are not always one and the same, but are changed according to the order of spirits that are to be called, their places, times, hours; for in making a circle it ought to be considered in what time of the year, what day, and to what star or region they belong, and what functions they have: therefore to begin, let there be made three circles of the latitude of nine feet distant one from another about a hands breadth. First, write in the middle circle the name of the hour wherein you do the work; in the second place, write the name of the angel of the hour, in the third place, the seal of the spirit of the hour; fourthly, the name of the spirit that rules the day in which you work, and the names of his ministers; in the fifth place, the name of the present time; sixthly, the name of the spirits ruling in that part of time, and their presidents; seventhly, the name of the head of the sign ruling in the time; eightly, the name of the earth, according to the time of working; ninthly, and for the completing of the middle circle, write the names of the sun and moon, according to the said rule of time: for as the times are changed, so are the names; and in the outer circle let there be drawn, in the four angles, the names of the great presidential spirits of the air that day wherein you would do this work, viz. the name of the king and his three ministers. Without the circle, in four angles, let pentagons be made. In the inner circle write four divine names, with four crosses interposed: in the middle of the circle, viz: towards the east let be written Alpha; towards the west, Omega; and let a cross divide the middle of the circle.

When the circle is thus finished, according to rule you shall proceed to consecrate and bless it saying:

In the name of the holy, blessed, and glorious trinity, proceed we to our work in these mysteries to accomplish that which we desire; we therefore, in the names aforesaid, consecrate this piece of ground for our defence, so that no spirit whatsoever shall be able to break these boundaries, neither be able to cause injury nor detriment to any of us here assembled; but that they be compelled to stand before this circle, and answer truly our demands, as far as it pleaseth him who liveth for ever and ever; and who says, I am Alpha and Omega, the Beginning and the End, which is, and was, living and was dead: and behold that I live for ever and ever; and I have the keys of death and hell. Bless, O Lord! this creature of earth wherein we stand; confirm, O God! thy strength in us, so that neither the adversary nor any evil thing may cause us to fail, through the metis of Jesus Christ, Amen.

It is also to be known that the spirits rule the hours in a successive order, according to the course of the heavens and the planets to which they are subject; so the same spirit which governeth the day rules also the first hour of the day; the second from this governs the second hour, and so on throughout; and when seven planets and hours have made their revolution it returns again to the first which rules the day. Therefore we shall first speak of the names of the hours, viz.

TABLE SHOWING THE MAGICAL NAMES OF THE HOURS, BOTH DAY AND NIGHT

	Names of hours of the day.		Names of hours of the Night.
1	Yain	1	Beron
2	Janor	2	Barol
3	Nasnia	3	Thami
4	Salla	4	Athar
5	Sededadi	5	Methon
6	Thamur	6	Rana
7	Ourer	7	Netos
8	Thamic	8	Tafrac
9	Neron	9	Sassur
10	Jayon	10	Agle
11	Abai	11	Calerva
12	Natalon	12	Salam

Of the names of the angels and their seals it shall be spoken in their proper places; but here we will show the names of the times.

A year therefore is four-fold, and is divided into spring, summer, autumn, and winter; the names thereof are these:

The spirit, **Talvi**; the summer, **Casmaran**; the autumn, the winter, **Farlas**.

The Angels of the Spring,—**Caracasa, Core, Amatiel, Comissoros.**

The head of the sign in spring is, **Spugliguel.**
The name of the earth in spring, **Amadai.**
The names of the sun and the moon in spring:
sun, **Abraym**; moon, **Augusita.**
The Angels of the Summer—**Gargatel, Tariel, Gaviel.**
The head of the sign of summer, **Tubiel.**
The name of the earth in summer, **Festativi.**
The names of the sun and moon in summer:
sun, **Athemay**; moon, **Armatus.**
The Angels of the Autumn—**Tarquam, Guabarel.**
The head of the sign of autumn, **Torquaret.**
The name of the earth in autumn, **Rabinnara.**
The names of the sun and moon in autumn: the
sun, **Abragini**; the moon, **Matasignais.**
The Angels of the Winter—**Amabael, Cetarari.**
The head of the sign of winter, **Attarib.**
The name of the earth in winter, **Geremiah.**
The names of the sun and moon in winter: the
sun, **Commutoff**; the moon, **Affaterim.**

These things being known, finish the consecration of the circle by saying:—

"Thou shalt purge me with hysop, O Lord, and I shall be clean: thou shalt wash me and I shall be whiter than snow."

Then sprinkle the same with holy water, and proceed with the benediction of the perfumes.

BENEDICTION OF PERFUMES

The God of Abraham, God of Isaac, God of Jacob, bless here the creatures of these kinds, that they may fill up the power and virtue of their odours; so that neither the enemy nor any false imagination may be able to enter into them; through our Lord Jesus Christ, &c. Then sprinkle the same with holy water.

THE EXORCISM OF FIRE INTO WHICH THE
PERFUMES ARE TO BE PUT

I exorcise thee, O thou creature of fire, by the only true God Jehovah, Adonai, Tetragrammaton, that forthwith thou cast away every phantasm from thee, that it shall do no hurt to any one. We beseech thee, O Lord to bless this creature of fire and sanctify it, so that it may be blessed to set forth the praise and glory of thy holy name, and that no hurt may be permitted to come to the exorciser or spectators; through our Lord Jesus Christ. Amen.

OF THE PENTACLE OF THE HINDU

It is always necessary to have this pentacle in readiness to bind with, in case the spirits would refuse to be obedient, as they can have no power over the exorcist while provided with and fortified by the pentacle the virtue of the holy names therein written presiding with wonderful influence over the spirits.

It should be made in the day and hour of Mercury upon parchment made of a kidskin, or virgin, or pure, clean, white paper; and the figures and letters wrote in pure gold; and it ought to be consecrated and sprinkled with holy water.

When the vesture is put on, it will be convenient to say the following oration:—

An Oration when the Habit or Vesture is put on

Anoor, Amacor, Amides, Theodonias, Anitor; by the merits of the angels, O Lord! I will put on the garment of salvation, that this which I desire I may bring to effect, through thee, the most holy Adonai, whose kingdom endureth for ever and ever. Amen.

THE MANNER OF WORKING

Let the moon be increasing and equal, if it can then be conveniently done; but especially let her not be combust, or in via combusts, which is between fourteen degrees of Libra and fourteen degrees of Scorpio.

The disciple must be clean and purified for nine days before he does the work. Let him have ready the perfume appropriated to the day wherein he does the work; and he must be provided with holy water from an Adept, or he may make it holy himself, by reading over it the consecration of water of baptism; he must have a new vessel of earth, with fire, the vesture, and the pentacle; and let all these things be rightly and duly consecrated and prepared. Let one of the companions carry the vessel with fire, and the perfumes, and let another bear the book, the garment, and pentacle; and let the operator himself carry the sword, over which should be said a prayer of consecration: and on the middle of the sword on one side let there be engraven Agla, and on the other side, Tetragrammaton. And the place being fixed upon where the circle is to be erected let him draw the lines we have before taught, and sprinkle the same with holy water, consecrating, etc., etc.

The disciple must therefore be prepared with fasting, chastity, and abstinence, for the space of three days before the day of operation; and on the day that he would do this work, being clothed with the forementioned vesture, and furnished with pentacles perfumes, a sword, bible, paper, pen, and consecrated ink, and all things necessary hereunto let him enter the circle, and call the angels from the four parts of the world, which do rule the seven planets, the seven days of the week, colours, and metals, whose names you will see in their places; and, with bended knees first let him say the Paterposter or Lord's Prayer, and then let him invocate the said angels, saying: —

O angeli, supradicti estote adjutores mihi petitioni and in adjutorum mihi in meis rebus et petitionibus.

Then call the angels from the four parts of the world that rule the air the same day in which he makes the experiment: and, having employed especially all the names and spirits within the circle, say:—

O vos omnes, adjutore atque contestor per sedem Adonai, per Hagios, Theos, Lschyros, Athanatos, Paracletos, Alpha and Omega, and per hoec tria nomina secreta, Agla. On, Tetragrammaton, quod hodie debeatis adimplere quod cupio.

These things being performed, let him read the conjuration assigned for the day; but if they shall be pertinacious or refractory, and will not yield themselves obedient, neither to the conjuration assigned for the day, nor any of the players before made, then use the exorcism followin!—

A General Exorcism of the Spirits of the Air

We being made after the image of God, endued with power from God and made after his will, do exorcise you by the most mighty and powerful name of God, El, strong and wonderful, (here name the spirit which is to appear), and we command you by Him who spoke the word and it was done, and by all the names of God, and by the name Adonai, El, Elohim, Elohe, Zebaoth, Elion, Eservhie, Jah, Rejpore-Kogus, Sadai, Lord God Most High: we exorcise you, and powerfully command you that you forthwith appear unto us here before the circle in a fair human shape, without any deformity or tortuosity; come ye all such, because we command you by the name of Yaw and Vau, which Adam heard and spoke; and by the name of God, Agla, which Lot heard, and was saved with his family; and by the name Joth, which Jacob heard from the angel wrestling with him, and was delivered from the hand of his brother Esau; the name Zebaoth, which Moses named, and all the rivers were turned into blood; and by the name Eserchie Oriston, which Moses named, and all the rivers brought forth frogs, and they ascended into the houses of the Egyptians, destroying all things; and by the name Elion, which Moses named, and there was great hail, such as had not been since the beginning of the world; and by the name Adonai; which Moses named, and there came up locusts, which appeared upon the whole land of Egypt, and devoured all which the hail had left; and by the name Schema Amathia, which Joshua called upon, and the sun stayed his course; and by the name Alpha and Omega, which Daniel named, and destroyed Bel and slew the dragon; and in the name Emmanuel, which the three children, Sidrach, Misach, and Abednego sung in the midst of the fiery furnace, and were delivered; and by the name Hagios; and by the seal of Adonai, and by Ischyros, Athanatos,

Paracletos; and by these three secret names, Agla, On, Rejpore-Kogus, I do adjure and contest you; and by these names, and by all other names of the living and true God, our Lord Almighty, I exorcist you and command you, by Him who spoke the word and it was done, to whom all creatures are obedient; and by the dreadful judgment of God; and by the uncertain sea of glass that is before the divine Majesty, mighty, and powerful; by the four beasts before this throne, having eyes before and behind; and by the fire round about his throne; and by the holy angels of heaven; by the mighty wisdom of God, I do powerfully exorcise you, that you appear here before this circle, to fulfill our will in all things which shall seem good unto us; by the seal of Baldachia, and by this name Primeumaton, which Moses named, and the earth opened and swallowed up Corah, Dathan, and Abiram: and in the power of that name Primeumaton, commanding the whole host of heaven, we curse you, and deprive you of your office, joy, and place, and do bind you in the depth of the bottomless pit, there to remain until the dreadful day of the last judgment; and we bind you into eternal fire, and into the lake of fire and brimstone, unless you forthwith appear before this circle to do our will: therefore, come ye, by these names, Adonai, Zebaoth, Adonai, Amioram; come ye, come ye, come ye, Adonai commandeth; Saday, the most mighty King of Kings, whose power no creature is able to resist, be unto you most dreadful, unless ye obey, and forthwith affably appear before this circle, let miserable ruin and fire unquenchable remain with you; therefore come ye, in the name of Adonai, Zebaoth, Adonai, Amionai, Amioram; come, come, why stay you? Basten, Adonai, Sadai the King of Kings commands you: El, Aty, Titcip, Azia, Hin, Jen, Minosel, Achadan, Vay, Vaan, Ey, Exe, A, El, El, El A, Hy, Hau, Hau, Hau, Vau, Vau, Vau, Yau.

A Prayer to God, to be said in the four Parts of the World in the Circle

Amorule, Taneha, Latisten, Rabur, Theneba, Latisten, Sscha, Aladia, Alpha and Omega, Leyste, Orison, Adonai; O most merciful heavenly Father! have mercy upon me although a sinner; make appear the arm of thy power in me this day against these obstinate spirits, that I by thy will, may be made a contemplator of thy divine works, and may be illustrated with all wisdom, to the honour and glory of thy holy name. I humbly beseech thee, that these spirits which I call by thy judgment may be bound and constrained to come and give true and perfect answers to those things which I shall ask of them; and that they may do and declare those thing unto us, which by me may be commanded of them, not hurting any creature, neither injuring or terrifying me of my fellows, nor hurting any other creature, and affrighting no man; and let them be obedient to those things which are required of them.

Then, standing in the middle of the circle, stretch out thy hand towards the pentacle, saying, by the pentacle of Solomon I have called you; give me a true answer.

Then follow this Oration—

Beralanensis, Balachienses, Paumachia and Apologia Sedes, by the most mighty kings and powers, and the most powerful princes, genii, Liachidae, ministers of the Tartarean seat, chief prince of the seat of Apologia, in the ninth legion, I invoke you, and by invocating, conjure you; and being armed with power from the supreme Majesty, I strongly command you, by Him who spoke and it was done, and to whom all creatures are obedient; and by the ineffable name, Tetragrammaton Jehovah, which being heard the elements are overthrown, the air is shaken, the sea runneth back, the fire is quenched, the earth trembles, and all the host of the celestials, and terrestials, and infernald do tremble together, and are troubled and confounded: wherefore, forthwith and without delay, do you come from all parts of the world, and make rational answers unto all things I shall ask of you; and come ye peaceably, visibly and affably now, without delay, manifesting what we desire, being conjured by the name of the living and true God, Helioren, and fulfill our commands, and persist unto the end, and according to our intentions, visibly and affably speaking unto us with a clear voice, intelligible, and without any ambiguity.

91

OF THE APPEARANCE OF THE SPIRITS

These things being duly performed, there will appear infinite visions, apparitions, phantasms, etc., beating of drums, and the sound of all kinds of musical instruments; which is done by the spirits, that with the terror they might force some of the companions out of the circle, because they can effect nothing against the exorcist himself: after this you shall see an infinite company of archers, with a great multiple of horrible beasts, which will arrange themselves as if they would devour the companions; nevertheless, fear nothing.

Then the exorcist, holding the pentacle in his hand, let him say, "Avoid hence these iniquities, by the virtue of the banner of God." Then will the spirits be compelled to obey the exorcist, and the company shall see them no more.

Then let the exorcist, stretching out his hand with the pentacle say, "Behold the pentacle of Solomon, which I have led into your presence; behold the person of the exorcist in the middle of the exorcism, who is armed by God, without fear, and well provided, who potently invocateth and calleth you by exorcising; come, therefore, with speed, by the virtue of these names; Aye Saraye, Aye Saraye; defer not to come, by the eternal names of the living and true God, Eloy, Archima, Rabur, and by the pentacle of Solomon here present, which powerfully reigns over you; and by the virtue of the celestial spirits, your lords; and by the person of the exorcist, in the middle of the exorcism; being conjured, make haste and come, and yield obedience to your master, who is called Octinomos. This world, and then immediately you shall see great motions; which when you see, say, why stay you? Wherefore do you delay? What do you? Prepare yourselves to be obedient to your master in the name of the Lord, Bathat or Vachat rushing upon Abrac, Abeor, coming upon Aberer.

Then they will immediately come in their proper forms; and when you see them before the circle, show them the pentacle covered with fine linen; uncover it, and say, Behold your confusion if you refuse to be obedient; and suddenly they will appear in a peaceable form, and will say, Ask what you will, for we are prepared to fulfil all your commands, for the Lord hath subjected us hereunto.

Then let the exorcist say, Welcome spirits, or most noble princes. because I have called you through Him to whom every knee doth bow, both of things in heaven, and things in earth, and things under the earth; in whose hands are all the kingdoms of kings, neither is there any able to contradict his Majesty. Wherefore, I bind that you remain affable and visible before this circle, so long and so constant; neither shall you depart without my license, until you have truly and without any fallacy performed my will, by virtue of his power who hath set the sea her bounds, beyond which it cannot pass, nor go beyond the law of his providence, viz., of the Most High God, Lord, and King, who hath created all things. Amen.

Then let the exorcist mention what he would have done.

After which say, in the name of the Father, and of the Son, and of the Holy Ghost, go in peace unto your places; peace be between us and you; be ye ready to come when you are called.

HERE FOLLOW THE CONSIDERATIONS AND CONJURATIONS FOR EVERY DAY IN THE WEEK; AND FIRST OF THE CONSIDERATIONS, ETC.
OF SUNDAY

The angels of the Lord's day—**Michael, Dardiel, Huratapel.**

The angels of the air ruling on the Lord's day, **Varcan,** the king;—his ministers, **Tus, Andas, Cynabal.**

The wind which the angels of the air are said to rule, is the north wind.

The angels of the fourth heaven ruling on the Lord's day, which should be called from the four parts of the world, are,—east, **Samael, Baciel, Abel, Gabriel, Vionatraba:**—from the west, **Anael, Pabel, Ustael, Burchat, Suceratos, Capabili;**—from the north, **Aiel, Ariel, vel Aquiel, Masgabriel, Saphiel, Matuyel,**—at the south, **Haludie, Machasiel, Charsiel, Uriel, Naromiel.**

The perfume of Sunday is **Red Sanders.**

THE CONJURATION FOR SUNDAY

I conjure and confirm upon you, ye strong and holy angels of God, in the name of Adonai, Eye, Eye, Eya, which is he who was, and is, and is to come, Eye, Abray; and in the name Saday, Cados, Cados, sitting on high upon the cerubim; and by the great name of God himself, strong and powerful, who is exalted above all the heavens; Eye, Saraye, who created the world, the heavens, the earth, the seal, and all that in them is, in the first day, and sealed them with his holy name, Phaa; and by the name of the angels who rule in the fourth heaven, and serve before the most mighty Salamia, an angel great and honourable; and by the name of his star, which is Sol, and by his sign and by the immense name of the living God, and by all the names aforesaid, I conjure thee, O Michael, O great angel! who art chief ruler of this day; and by the name Adonai, the God of Isreal, I conjure thee, O Michael! that thou labour for me, and fulfill all my petitions according to my will and desire in my cause and business.

The spirits of the air of the Lord's day are under the north wind; their nature is to procure gold, gems, carbuncles, diamonds, and rubies, and to cause one to obtain favour and benevolence, to dissolve enmities amongst men, to raise honours, and to take away infirmities. They appear, for the most part, in a large, full and great body, sanguine and gross, in a gold heaven; the sign of their becoming visible is that they move the person to sweat that calls them; but their particular forms are as follows; viz.

A king, having a scepter, riding on a lion.

A king crowned; a queen with a scepter.

A bird; a lion; a cock.

A yellow garment.

A scepter.

CONSIDERATIONS ETC. OF MONDAY

The angels of Monday—**Gabriel, Michael, Samael.**

The angels of the air ruling Monday, **Arcan,** king;— his ministers, **Bilet, Missabu, Abuhaza.** The wind which these are subject to is the west wind.

The angels of the first heaven, ruling on Monday, to be called from the four parts of the world. From the east, **Gabriel, Madiel, Deamiel, Janak;**—from the west, **Sachiel, Zaniel, Habiel, Bachanoe, Corobael;**—from the north, **Mael, Uvael, Darquiel, Hanun, Vetuel.**

The perfume of Monday—Aloes.

THE CONJURATION OF MONDAY

I conjurn and confirm upon you, ye strong and good angels, in the name Adonai, Adonai, Adonai, Eye, Eye Eye; Cados, Cados, Cados, Achim, Achim, Ja, Ja, strong Ja, who appeared in mount Sinai with the glorification of king Adonai, Sadai, Zebaoth, Anathay, Ya, Ya, Ya, Maranata, Abim, Jeia, who created the sea, and all lakes and waters, in the second day, which are above the heavens, and in the earth, and sealed the sea in his name, and gave in its bounds beyond which it cannot pass; and by the names of the angels who rule in the first legion, and who serve Orphaniel, a great, precious, and honourable angel, and by the name of his star which is Luna, and by all the names aforesaid, I conjure thee, Gabriel, who are chief ruler of Monday, the second day, that for me thou labour and fulfill, etc.

The spirits of the air of Monday are subject to the west wind, which is the wind of the moon; their nature is to give silver and to convey things from place to place; to make horses swift, and to disclose the secrets of persons both present and future.

Their familiar Forms are as follows:—

They appear generally of a great and full stature, soft and phlegmatic, of colour like a black, obscure cloud, having swolen countenance, with eyes red and full of water, a bald head, and teeth like a wild boar; their motion is like an exceeding great tempest of the sea. For their sign there will appear an exceeding great rain, and their particular shapes are:—

A king like an archer, riding upon a doe.
A little boy.
A woman-hunter with a bow and arrows.
A sow; a little doe; a goose.
A green, or silver-coloured garment.
An arrow; a creature with many feet.

CONSIDERATIONS OF TUESDAY

The angels of the air on Tuesday—**Samael, Satael, Amabiel.**

The angels of the air ruling on Tuesday—**Samax,** king; his ministers,—**Carmax, Ismoli, Paffran.**

The wind to which the said angels are subject is the east wind.

The angels of the fifth heaven ruling on Tuesday,—at the east,—**Friagne, Guel, Damael, Calzas, Arrangon;**—the west, **Lama, Astagna, Lobquin, Soneas, Jazel, Lsiael, Irel;**—the north, **Rhaumek, Hyniel, Rayel, Seraphiel, Fraciel, Mathiel;**—the south, **Sacriel, Janiel, Galdel, Osael, Vianuel, Zaliel.**

The perfume of Tuesday—Pepper.

THE CONJURATION OF TUESDAY

I conjure and call upon you, ye strong and good angels, in the names Ya, Ya, Ya; He, He, He; Va, Hy, Hy, Ha, Ha, Ha; Va, Va, Va; An, An, An; Aia, Aia, Aia; El, Ty, Elibra, Elohim, Elohim; and by the names of the High God who hath made the sea and dry land, and by his word hath made the earth, produced trees, and hath set his seal upon the planets, with his precious, honoured, revered and holy name; and by the names of the angels governing in the fifth house, who are subservient to the great angel Acimony, who is strong and powerful, also honoured, and by the name of his star which is called Mars, I call upon thee, Samael, by the names above mentioned, thou great angel! who presides over the day of Mars, and by the name Adonai, the living and true God, that you assit me in accomplishing my labours, etc. (as in the conjuration for Sunday.)

The spirits of the air on Tuesday are under the east wind; their nature is to bring or cause war, mortality, death, combustions, and to give two-thousand soldiers at a time; to bring death, infirmity or health.

Familiar Forms of the Spirits of Mars

They appear in a tall body and choleric, a filthy countenance, of colour brown, swarthy, or red, having horns

96

like harts, and griffins claws, and bellowing like wild bulls. Their motion is like fire burning: their sign thunder and lightning round about the crcle.

Their particular shapes are, a king armed, riding on a wolf; a man armed.

A woman with a buckler on her thight.

A she-goat; a horse; a stag.

A red garment; a pieve of wool; a cowslip.

CONSIDERATIONS OF WEDNESDAY

The angels of Wednesday—**Raphael, Meil Seraphiel.**

The angels of the air ruling on Wednesday, **Mediat,** King; his ministers, **Suquinos, Sallales;** the said angels of the air are subject to the south-west wind.

The angels of the second heaven, governing Wednesday, that are to be called, etc. At the east—**Mathlai, Tarmiel, Baraborat,**—at the west, **Jeruscue, Merattron;** at the north, **Thiel, Rael, Jarihael, Venahel, Velel, Abuiori, Ucimiel,**—at the south, **Milliel, Nelapa, Calvel, vel Laquel.**

THE CONJURATION OF WEDNESDAY

I conjure and call upon you, ye strong and holy angels, good and powerful, in a strong name of fear and praise, Ja, Adonai, Elohim, Saday, Saday, Saday; Eie, Eie, Eie; Asamie, Asamie; and in the name of Adonai, the God of Israel, who hath made the two great lights and distinguish day from night, for the benefit of his creatures; and by the names of all the discerning angels, governing openly in the second house before the great angel, Tetra, strong and powerful; and by the name of his star which is Mercury; and by the name of his seal, which is that of a powerful and honoured God; and I call upon thee, Raphael, and by the names above mentioned, thou great angel who presidest over the fourth day; and by the holy name which is written in the front of Aaron, created the most high priest, and by the names of all the angels who are constant in the grace of Christ, and by the name and place of Ammalium, that you assist me in my labours, etc., etc.

The spirits of the air, on Wednesday are subject to the south-west wind; their nature is to give all sorts of metals, to reveal all earthly things past, present, and to come; to pacify judges, to give victory in war, to teach experiments, and all sciences decayed, and to change bodies mixed of elements conditionally, out of one thing into another; to give health or infirmities, to raise the poor and cast down the rich, to bind or loose spirits, to open locks or bolts.

Such kinds of spirits have the operation of others but not in their perfect power, but in virtue of knowledge.

Forms of the Spirits of Mercury

The spirits of Mercury appear in a body of a middle stature, cold, liquid and moist, fair and of an affable speech in a human shape and form, like a knight armed, of colour clear and bright. The motion of them is like silver coloured clouds: for their sign they cause horror and fear to him that calls them.

Their particular shapes are, a king riding upon a bear.

A fair youth; a woman holding a distaff.

A dog; a she-bear; and a magpye.

A garment of various changeable colours.

A rod; a little staff.

CONSIDERATIONS OF THURSDAY

The angels of Thursday—**Saciel, Cassiel, Asasiel.**

The angels of tne air of Thursday,—**Suth,** king; ministers, **Maguth, Gutrix.**

The angels of the air are under the south wind—(But because there are no angels of the air to be found above the fifth heaven, therefore, on Thursday, say the prayers following in the four parts of the world:) At the east— O Deus magne et excelse et honorate, per infinita secula; O great and most high God, honoured by the name, world without end. At the west—O wise, pure and just God, of divine clemency, I beseech thee, most holy Father, that this day I may perfectly understand and accomplish my petition, work and labour; for the honour and glory of thy holy name, who livest and reignest, world without end. Amen. At the north—O God, strong, mighty and wonderful, from everlasting to everlasting, grant that this day I bring to effect that which I desire, through our blessed Lord. Amen. At the south—O mighty and most merciful God, hear my prayers and grant my petition.

The perfume of Thursday—Saffron.

THE CONJURATION OF THURSDAY

I conjure and confirm upon you, ye strong and holy angels, by the names Sados, Cados, Cados, Eschereie, Eschereie, Eschereie, Hatim, Ya, strong founder of the worlds; Cantine, Jaym, Janic, Anic, Calbot, Sabbac, Berisay, Alnaym, and by the name Adonai, who created fishes and creeping things in the waters, and birds upon the face of the earth, flying towards heaven, in the fifth day; and by the names of the angels serving in the sixth host before Pastor, a holy angel and a great and powerful prince, and by the name of his star, which is Jupiter, and by the name of his seal, and by the name of Adonai, the great God, Creator of all things, and by the name of all the stars, and by their power and virtue, and by all the names aforesaid, I conjure thee, sachiel, a great Angel. who art chief ruler of Thursday, that for me thou labour etc.

The spirits of the air of Thursday are subject to the south wind; their nature is to procure the love of women, to cause men to be merry and joyful, to pacify strifes and contentions, to appease enemies. to heal the diseased, and to disease the whole and procure losses, or restore things lost.

The Familiar Forms of the Spirits of Jupiter

They appear with a body sanguine and choleric, of a middle stature, with a horrible, fearful motion, but with a mild countenance, and a gentle speech, and of the colour of iron: the motion of them is flashings of lightning and thunder. For their sign there will appear about the circle men who shall seem to be devoured by lions. Their forms are:—

A king, with a sword drawn, riding on a stag.

A man, wearing a mitre, with long raiment.

A maid, with a laurel crown, adorned with flowers.

A bull; a stag; a peacock.

An azure garment; a sword; a boxtree.

99

CONSIDERATIONS OF FRIDAY

The angels of Friday—**Annael, Rachiel, Sachiel.**
The angels of the air ruling on Friday, **Sarabotes,** king; ministers, **Amahiel, Aba, Abalidoth, Blaef.** The wind which the angels of the air is subject to is the west wind.

Angels of the third heaven, which are to be called from the four parts of the world, are:—at the east, **Setchiel, Chedusitanick, Corat, Tamuel, Tenaciel;**—at the west, **Turiel, Coniel, Babiel, Kadie, Maltiel, Huphaltiel;**—at the north, **Sachiel, Chermiel, Samael, Santanael, Famiel.**

The perfume of Friday—Papperwort.

THE CONJURATIONS OF FRIDAY

I conjure and confirm upon you, ye strong and holy angels by the names On, Hey, Heya, Ja, Je, Saday, Adonai, and in the name Sadai, who created four-footed beasts, and creeping things, and man, in the sixth day, and gave to Adam power over all creatures; wherefore blessed be the name of the Creator in his place; and by the name of the angels serving in the third host, before Dagiel, a great angel, and a strong and powerful prince, and by the name of his star, which is Venus, and by his seal which is holy; and by all names aforesaid, I conjure upon thee, Anael, who are chief ruler this day, that thou labour for me, &c.

The spirits of the air on Friday are subject to the west wind; their nature is to give silver, to incite men, and incline them to luxury, to cause marriages, to allure men to love women, to cause or take away infirmities, and to do all things which have motion.

Their Familiar Shapes

They appear with a fair body, of middle stature, with an amiable and pleasant countenance, of colour white or green, their upper parts golden; the motion of them is like a clear star. For their sign there will appear naked virgins round the circle, which will strive to allure the invocator to dalliance with them: but—

100

Their Particular Shapes Are:—

A king, with a scepter, riding on a camel.

A naked girl; a she goat.

A camel; a dove.

A white or green garment.

Flowers; the herb savine.

THE CONSIDERATIONS OF SATURDAY

The angels of the air ruling this day, **Maymon, king;** Ministers, **Abumalith, Assaibi, Balidet.** The wind they are subject to, the south wind.

The fumigation of Saturday is Sulphur.

There are no angels ruling in the air on Saturday above the fifteen heaven, therefore in the four corners of the world, in the circle, use these oration which are applied to Thursday.

THE CONJURATION OF SATURDAY

I conjure and confirm upon you, Caphrie, or Cassiel, Machator, and Seraquiel, strong and powerful angels; and by the name Adonai, Adonai, Adonai; Eie, Eie, Eie; Acim, Acim, Acim; Cados, Cados; Ima, Ima, Ima, Salay, Ja, Sar, Lord and Maker of the world, who rested on the 7th day; and by him who of his good pleasure gave the same to be observed by the children of Israel throughout their generations, that they should keep and sanctify the same, to have thereby a good reward in the world to come; and by the names of the angels serving in the seventh host, before Booel, a great angel, and powerful prince; and by the name of his star, which is Saturn; and by his holy seal, and by the names before spoken, I conjure upon thee, Caphriel, who art chief ruler of the seventh day, which is the Sabbath, that for thou labour, etc., etc.

The spirits of the air on Saturday are subject to the south-west wind; the nature of them is to sow discords, hatred, evil thoughts and cogitations, to give leave to kill and murder, and to lame or main every member.

Their Familiar Shapes

They generally appear with a tall, lean, slender body, with an angry countenance, having four faces, one on the back of the head, one in the front, and one on each side, nosed or beaked, likewise there appears a face on each knee of a black shining colour; their motion is the moving of the wind, with a kind of earthquake; their sign in white earth, whiter than snow.

Their Particular Shapes Are:—

A king bearded, riding on a dragon.

An old man with a beard.

An old woman leaning on a crutch.

A hog, a dragon; an owl.

A black garment; a hook or sickle.

A juniper tree.

These are the figures that these spirits usually assume, which are generally terrible at the first coming on of the visions, but as they have only a limited power, beyond which they cannot pass, so the invocator need be under no apprehensions of danger, provided he is well fortified with those things we have directed to be used for his defence, and above all, to have a firm and constant faith in the mercy, wisdom, and goodness of God.

LIST OF ANGELS, SPIRITS, DEMONS, GOBLINS AS COMPILED BY
LEWIS de CLARMÓNT

ABBADON:

(The Destroyer.) Chief of the demons of the seventh hierarchy. Addaddon is the name given by St. John in the Apocalypse to the king of the grasshoppers. He is sometimes regarded as the destroying angel.
Candle No. 21; Incense No. 3; Oil No. 5.

ABIGOR:

According to Wierius (q. v.), the Grand Duke of Hades, he is shown in the form of a handsome knight, bearing lance, standard, or sceptre. He is a demon of the superior order and responds readily to questions concerning war. He can foretell the future, and instructs the leaders how to make themselves respected by the soldiers. Sixty of the infernal regions are at his command.
Candle No. 2; Incense No. 5; Oil No. 8.

ADDANC OF THE LAKE:

A monster that figures in the Mabinogi legend of Peredur. Peredur obtains a magic stone which renders him invisible, and he thus succeeds in slaying this monster, which had daily killed the inhabitants of the palace of the King of Tortures.
Candle No. 1; Incense No. 9; Oil No. 3.

ADHAB-ALGAL:

The Mohammedan purgatory, where the wicked are tormented by the dark angels Munkir and Nekir.
Candle No. 3 and No. 4; Incense No. 9; Oil No. 2.

ADONAI:

A Hebrew word signifying, "the Lord," and used by the Hebrews when speaking or writing of Jehovan, the awful and ineffable name of the God of Israel. The Jews entertained the deepest awe for this incommunicable and mysterious name, and this feeling led them to avoid pronouncing it and to the substitution of the word Adonai for

"Jehovan" in their sacred text. This custom still prevails among the Jews, who attribute to—the pronouncement of the Holy Name the power of working miracles. The Jehovah of the Israelites was their invisible protector and king, and no image of him was made. He was worshipped according to his commandments, with an observance of ritual instituted through Moses. The term "Jehovah" means the revealed Absolute Deity, the Manifest, Only Personal Holy Creator and Redeemer.

Candle No. 30; Incense No. 7; Oil No. 6.

ADRAMELECH:

According to Wierius (q. v.) Chancellor of the infernal regions, Keeper of the Wardrobe of the Demon King, and President of the High Council of the Demon Kings. He was worshipped at Sepharvaim, and Assyrian town, where children were burned on his altar. The rabbis say that he shows himself in the form of a mule, or sometimes, of a peacock.

Candle No. 5; Incense No. 6; Oil No. 9.

AGABERTE:

Daughter of a certain giant called Vagnoste, dwelling in Scandinavia. She was a powerful enchantress, and was rarely seen in her true shape. Sometimes she would take the form of an old woman, wrinkled and bent, and hardly able to move about. At one time she would appear weak and ill, and at another tall and strong, so that her head seemed to touch the clouds. These transformations she affected without the smallest effort or trouble. People were so struck with her marvels that they believed her capable of overthrowing the mountains, tearing up the trees, drying up the rivers with the greatest of ease. They held that nothing less than a legion of demons must be at her command for the accomplishment of her magic feats. She seems to be like the Scottish Caileach Bheur, a nature hag.

Candle No. 6; Incense No. 10; Oil No. 11.

AGARES:

According to Wierius (q. v.) Grand Duke of the eastern region of Hades. He is shown under the form of a benevolent lord mounted on a crocodile, and carrying a hawk on his fist. The army he protects in battle is indeed fortunate,

for he disperses their enemies, and puts new courage into the hearts of the cowards who fly before superior numbers. He distributes place and power, titles, and prelacies, teaches all languages, and has other equally remarkable powers. Thirty-one legions are under his command.
Candle No. 7; Incense No. 1; Oil No. 12.

AGATHION:

A familiar spirit which appears only at mid-day. It takes the shape of a man or a beast, or even encloses itself in a talisman, bottle or magic ring.
Candle No. 8; Incense No. 7; Oil No. 4.

AGATHODEMON:

A good demon, worshipped by the Egyptians under the shape of a serpent with a human head. The dragons or flying serpents venerated by the ancients were also called Agathodemons, or good genies.
Candle No. 9; Incense No. 2; Oil No. 10.

AHAZU-DEMON:

(The Seizer). Practically nothing is known of this Semitic demon unless it is the same Ahazie told of in medical texts, where a man can be stricken by a disease bearing this name.
Candle No. 21; Incense No. 4; Oil No. 1.

AHRIMANES:

The name given to the Chief of the Cacodaemons, of fallen angels, by the Persians and Chaldeans. These cacodaemons were believed to have been expelled from Heaven for their sins; they endeavoured to settle down in various parts of the earth, but were always rejected, and out of revenge they find their pleasure in injuring the inhabitants. Xenoritus thought that penance and self-mortification. though not agreeable to the gods, pacified the malice of the Cacodaemons. Ahrimanes and his followers finally took up their abodes in all the space between the earth and the fixed stars, and there established their domain, which is called Arhiman-abad. As Ahrimanes was the spirit of evil his counterpart in Persian dualism was Ormuzd, the creative and benevolent being.
Candle No. 41; Incense No. 4; Oil No. 13.

AKATHASO:

Evil spirits inhabiting trees.

Candle No. 10; Incense No. 2; Oil No. 15.

ALASTOR:

A cruel demon, who, according to Wierius, filled the post of chief executioner to the monarch of Hades. The conception of him somewhat resembles that of Nemesis. Zorquaster, is said to have called him "The Executioner. Others confound him with the destroying angel. Evil genies were formerly called Alastors. Plutarch says that Cicero, who bore a grudge against Augustus, conceived the plan of committing suicide on the emperor's hearth, and thus becoming his Alastor.

Candle No. 20; Incense No. 6; Oil No. 14.

ALBIGENSES:

A sect which originated in the south of France in the twelfth century. They were so called from one of their territorial centres, that of Albi. It is probable that their heresy came originally from Eastern Europe, and they were often designated Bulgarians, and undoubtedly kept up intercourse with certain secretaries of Thrace, the Bogomils; and they are sometimes connected with the Paulicians. It is difficult to form any exact idea of their doctrines, as Albigensian texts are rare, and contain little concerning their ethics, but we know, that they were strongly opposed to the Roman Catholic Church, and protested against the corruption of its clergy. But it is not as a religious body that we have to deal with the Albigenses here but to consider whether or not their cult possessed any occult significance. It has been claimed by their opponents that they admitted two fundamental principles, good and bad, saying that God had produced Lucifer from Himself; that indeed Lucifer was the son of God who revolted against Him, that he had carried with him, a rebelious party of angels, who were driven from Heaven along with him; that Lucifer in his exile had created this world with its inhabitants where he reigned, and where all was evil. It is alleged that they further believed that God for the re-establishment of order

OSIRIS

THE SPIRIT
ANTICHRIST.

had produced a second son, who was Jesus Christ. Further-more the Catholic writers on the Albigenses charged them with believing that the souls of men were demons lodged in mortal bodies in punishment of their crimes.

All this is, of course, mere tradition, and we may be sure that the dislike of the Albigenses for the irregularities then current in the Roman Church, brought such charges on the heads. They were indeed, the lineal ancestors of Protestantism. A crusade was brought against them by Pope Innocent III, and wholesale massacres took place. The Inquisition was also let loose upon them, and they were driven to hide in the forests and among the mountains, where, like the Covenanters of Scotland, they held surrep-titious meetings. The Inquisition terrorised the district in which they had dwelt so thoroughly that the very name of Albigenses was practically blotted out, and by the year 1330, the records of the Holy Office show no further writs issued against the heretics.

Candle No. 26; Incense No. 5; Oil No. 7.

ALBIGERIOUS:

A Carthaginian soothsayer mentioned by St. Augus-tine. He would fall into strange ecstacies in which his soul, separated from his body, would travel abroad and find out what was taking place in distant parts. He could read peo-ple's inmost thoughts, and discover anything he wished to learn. These wonders were ascribed to the agency of the Devil. St. Augustine also speaks of another case, in which the possessed man was ill of a fever; though not in a trance but wide awake, he saw the priest who was coming to visit him while he was yet six leagues away, and told the com-pany assembled round his couch the exact moment when the good man would arrive.

Candle No. 11; Incense No. 4; Oil No. 11.

ALDINACH:

An Egyptian demon whom the demonologists picture as presiding over the tempest, earthquakes, rain-storms, hail-storms, etc. It is he, also, who sinks ships. When he appears in visible form he takes the shape of a woman.

Candle No. 40; Incense No. 3; Oil No. 2.

ALLAT:

Wife of Allah, and joint ruler with him over the Chaldean Hell. M. Maspero describes as the "throne lady of the great country where all go after death who have breathed here below," and as their terrible judge.
Candle No. 18; Incense No. 7; Oil No. 1.

ALOCER:

A powerful demon, according to Wierius, Grand Duke of Hades. He appears in the shape of a knight mounted on an enormous horse. His face has leonine characteristics; he has a ruddy complexion and burning eyes; and he speaks with much gravity. He is said to give family happiness to those whom he takes under his protection, and to teach astronomy and liberal arts. Thirty-six legions are controlled by him.
Candle No. 12; Incense No. 9; Oil No. 12.

ALRUNES:

Female demons or sorceresses, the mothers of the Huns. They took all sorts of shapes, but without changing their sex. The name was given by the Germans to little statues of old sorceresses, about a foot high. To these they attributed great virtues, honouring them as the negroes honour their fetishes; clothing them richly, housing them comfortably, and serving them with food and drink at every meal. They believed that if these little images were neglected they would cry out, a catastrophe which was to be avoided at all costs, as it brought dire misfortunes upon the household. They may have been mandrakes and it was claimed for them that they could foretell the future, answering by means of motions of the head, or unintelligible words. They are still consulted in Norway.
Candle No. 39; Incense No. 1; Oil No. 15.

ALPIEL:

An angel or demon, who, according to the Talmud, presides over fruit-trees.
Candle No. 7; Incense No. 8; Oil No. 3.

ALU-DEMON:

This Semitic demon owes his parentage to a human being; he hides himself in caverns and corners, and slinks through the streets at night. He also lies in wait for the unwary, and at night enters bed-chambers and terrorises folks, threatening to pounce upon them if they shut their eyes.

Candle No. 4; Incense No. 10; Oil No. 4.

AMAIMON:

One of the four spirits who preside over the four parts of the universe. Amaimom, according to the magicians, was the governor of the eartern part.

Candle No. 41; Incense No. 12; Oil No. 6.

AMDUSCIAS:

Grand Duke of Hades. He has, according to Wierius (q. v.) the form of an unicorn, but when evoked, appears in human shape. He gives concerts, at the command of men, where one hears the sound of all the musical instruments but can see nothing. It is said that the trees themselves incline to his voice. He commands twenty-nine legions.

Candle No. 16; Incense No. 5; Oil No. 9:

Amon:

A great and powerful marquis of the infernal empire. He is represented as a wolf with a serpent's tail, vomiting flame. When he appears in human form, his head resembles that of a large owl with canine teeth. He is the strongest of the princes of demons, knows the past and the future and can reconcile, when he will friends who have quarrelled. He commands forty legions.

Candle No. 19; Incense No. 7; Oil No. 8.

AMOYMON:

One of the four kings of Hades of which the eastern part falls to his share. He may be invoked in the morning from nine o'clock till midday. and in the evening from three o'clock till six. He has been identified with Amaimon (q. v.) Asmodeus (q. v.) is his lieutenant and the first prince of his dominions.

Candle No. 27; Incense No. 3; Oil No. 10.

111

ANAMELECH:

An obscure demon, bearer of ill news. He was worshipped at Sepharvaun, a town of Assyrians. He always reveals himself in the figure of a quail. His name, we are told, signifies a "good king and some authorities declare that this demon is the moon, as Andramelech is the sun. Candle No. 28; Incense No. 9; Oil No. 14.

ANARAZEL:

One of the demons charged with the guardianship of subterranean treasures, which he carries about from one place to another, to hide them from men. It is he who, with his companions Gaxiel and Fecor, shakes the foundations of houses, raises the tempests, rings the bells at midnight, causes spectres to appear, and inpires a thousand terrors. Candle No. 22; Incense No. 6; Oil No. 13.

ANGELS:

Jehovah, attributed to God the Father, being the pure and simple essence of the divinity, flowing through Hajoth Hakados to the angel Metratton and to the ministering spirit, Reschith Hajalalim, who guides the primum mobile, and bestows the gift of being on all. These names are to be understood as pure essences, or as spheres of angels, and blessed spirits, by whose agency the divine providence extends to all his words.

Jah, attributed to the person of the Messiah or Logos, whose power and influence descends through the angel Masleh into this sphere of the Zodiac. This is the spirit or word that actuated the chaos, and ultimately produced the four elements, and all creatures that inherit them, by the agency of a spirit named Raziel, who was the ruler of Adam.

Ehjeh, attributed to the holy Spirit, whose divine light is received by the angel Sabbathi, and communicated from him through the sphere of Saturn. It denotes the beginning of the supernatural generation, and hence of all living souls. The ancient Jews considered the three superior names which are above, to be attributed to the divine essence as personal or proper names while the seven following denote the measure (middoth) or attributes which are invisible in the works of God. But the modern Jews, in opposition

112

A DECEIVER.

APOLLYON.

VESSELS OF IN GINTY.

to the tripersonalists, consider the whole as attributes. Maurice makes the worlds, to each of which a presiding angel was assigned.

El, strength, power, light, through which flow grace, goodness, mercy, piety, and munificence to the angel Zadkiel, and passing through the sphere of Jupiter fashioneth the images of all bodies, bestowing clemency, benevolence and justice on all.

Elohi, the upholder of the sword and left hand of God. Its influence penetrates the angel Geburah (or Gamaliel) descends through the sphere of Mars. It imparts fortitude in times of war and affliction.

Tsebaoth, the title of God as Lord of hosts. The angel is Raphael, through whom its mighty power passes into the sphere of the sun, giving motion, heat and brightness to it.

Elion, the title of God as the highest. The angel is Michael. The sphere to which it imparts its influence is Mercury, giving benightity, motion, and intelligence, with elegance and consonance of speech.

Adonai, master or lord, governing the angel Haniel, and the sphere of Venue.

Shaddai, the virtue of this name is conveyed by Cherubim to the angel Gabriel, and influences the sphere of the moon. It causes increase and decrease, and rules the protecting spirits.

Elohim, the source of knowledge, understanding and wisdom, received by the angel Jesodoth, and imparted to the sphere of the earth.
Candle No. 27; Incense No. 1; Oil No. 1.

AMMEBERG:

A demon of the mines, known principally in Germany. On one occasion he killed with his breath twelve miners who were working in a silver mine of which he had charge. He is a wicked and terrible demon, represented under the figure of a horse, with an immense neck and frightful eyes.
Candle No. 3; Incense No. 8; Oil No. 6.

ANPIEL:
One of the angels charged by the rabbis with the government of the birds, for every known species was put under the protection of one or more angels.
Candle No. 38; Incense No. 10; Oil No. 12.

ANSITIF:
A little known demon, who during the possession of the nuns of Louviers, in 1643 occupied the body of Sister Barbars of St. Michael.
Candle No. 25; Incense No. 4; Oil No. 2.

AONBARR:
A hores belonging to Manaanan, son of the Irish Sea-God, Lir. It was believed to possess magical gifts, and could gallop on land or sea.
Candle No. 14; Incense No. 5; Oil No. 3.

ARARIEL:
An angel who, according to the rabbis of the Talmud takes charge of the waters of the earth. Fisherman invoke him so that they may take large fish.
Candle No. 27; Incense No. 9; Oil No. 8.

ARAEL:
One of the spirits which the rabbis of the Talmud made prince and governor over the people of the birds.
Candle No. 37; Incense No. 3; Oil No. 4.

ARIOCH:
Demon of vengeance, according to some deomonologists. He is diefferent from Alastor, and occupies himself only with vengeance in particular cases where is employed for that purpose.
Candle No. 15; Incense No. 1; Oil No. 5.

ARIEL:
A spirit.
Candle No. 23; Incense No. 2; Oil No. 2.

ARDAT-LILE:
(Semitic Spirit). She is a female spirit or demon who weds human beings and works great harm in the dwellings of men.
Candle No. 28; Incense No. 7; Oil No. 7.

ARNUPHIS:

An Egyptian sorcerer who, seeing Marcus Aurelius and his army engaged in a pass whose entrance had been closed by their enemies,and dying of thirst under a burning sky, caused a miraculous rain to fall, which allowed the Romans to quench their thirst, while the thunder and hail obliged the enemy to give up their arms.
Candle No. 36; Incense No. 1; Oil No. 10.

ASAL:

Known as the King of the Golden Pillars, in Irish Celtic Myth. He was the owner of seven swine, which might be killed and eaten every night, yet were found alive every morning.
Candle No. 16; Incense No. 2; Oil No. 9.

ASIAH:

According to the Kabala, the first of the three classes or natural ranks among the spirits of men, who must advance from the lower to the higher.
Candle No. 29; Incense No. 3; Oil No. 8.

ASPILETTE:

(Marie d') : Witch of Andaye, in the country of Labour, who lived in the reign of Henry IV. She was arrested at the age of nineteen years, and confesses that she had been led to the "sabboth," and there made to perform diverse horrible rites.
Candle No. 35; Incense No. 4; Oil No. 7.

ASTOLPHO:

A hero of Italian romance. He was the son of Otho, King of England. He was transformed into a myrtle, by Alcina, a sorceress, but later regained his human form through sensuality.
Candle No. 17; Incense No. 3; Oil No. 6.

AUGUST SPIRITS:

The shelf of the: In the country of Japan, every house has a room set apart, called the spirit chamber in which there is a shelf or shrine, with tablets bearing the names of the deceased members of the family, with the sole addi-

tion of the word Mitana (spirit). This is a species of ancestor worship, and is known as "home" worship.
Candle No. 31; Incense No. 4; Oil No. 5.

AUSTATIKEO-PAULIGAUR:

A class of Persian evil spirits. They are eight in number, and keep the eight sides of the world. Their names are as follows:—(1) Indiren, the king of these genii; (2) AUGNE-BAUGAUVEN, the god of fire; (3) Eemen king of death and hell; (4) Nerudee, earth in the figure of a giant; (5) Vaivoo, god of the air and winds; (6) Varoonon, god of clouds and rain; (7) Gooberen, god of riches; (8) Essaunien, or Shivven.
Candle No. 18; Incense No. 3; Oil No. 4.

ANSUPEROMIN:

A sorcerer of the time of St. Jean de Lus, who, according to information supplied by Pierre Delamere, a councillor of Henry IV, was seen several times at the "sabboth" mounted on a demon in the shape of a goat, and playing on the flute for the witches' dance.
Candle No. 32; Incense No. 2; Oil No. 3.

AYPEROR:

A count of the infernal empire (The same as Ipes).
Candle No. 19; Incense No. 1; Oil No. 2.

AZAZEL:

A demon of the second order, guardian of the goat.
Candle No. 22; Incense No. 10; Oil No. 15.

AZER:

An angel of the elemental fire. Azer is also the name of the fathero f Zoroaster.
Candle No. 33; Incense No. 6; Oil No. 14.

BAALZEPHON:

Captain of the guard and sentinels of Hell, according to Wierius.
Candle No. 41; Incense No. 4; Oil No .9.

BACOTI:

A common name for the augurs and sorcerers of Tonquin. They are often consulted by the friends of deceased

persons for the purpose of holding communication with them.
Candle No. 2; Incense No. 3; Oil No. 7.

BAD:

A Jinn of Persia who is supposed to have command over the wind and tempests. He presides over the twenty-second day of the month.
Candle No. 1; Incense No. 2; Oil No. 9.

BAEL:

A demon cited in the Grand Grimoire (q. v.) and head of the infernal powers. It is with him that Wierius commences his inventory of the famous Pseudonomarchia Daemonum. He alludes to Beal as the first monarch of hell, and says that his estates are situated on the eastern regions thereof. He has three heads, one, that of a crab, another that of a cat, and the third that of a man. Sixty-six legions obey him.
Candle No. 20; Incense No. 5; Oil No. 2.

BAHAMAN:

A jinn who, according to Persian tradition, appeased anger, and in consequence governed oxen, sheep, and all animals of a peaceful disposition.
Candle No. 40; Incense No. 9; Oil No. 6.

BALAN:

A monarch great and terrible among the infernal powers, according to Wierius. He has three heads, those of a bull, a man, and a ram. Joined to these is the tail of a serpent, the eyes of which burn with fire. He bestrides an enormous bear. He commands forty of the infernal regions, and rules over finesse, ruses, and middle courses.
Candle No. 22; Incense No. 7; Oil No. 1.

BALTAZO:

One of the demons who possessed a young woman of Laon, Nicole Aubry, in the year 1566. He went to sup with her husband, under the pretext of freeing her from demon-possession, which he did not accomplish. It was observed that at supper he did not drink water which shows that demons are averse to water.
Candle No. 2; Incense No. 9; Oil No. 14.

BAR-LGURA:

(Semitic Demon): Sits on the roofs of houses and leaps on the inhabitants. People so afflicted are called d'abaregara.
Candle No. 20; Incense No. 3; Oil No. 9.

BARQU:

A demon in whose keeping was the secret of the Philosopher's stone.
Candle No. 19; Incense No. 3; Oil No. 12.

BARQUEST:

The: A goblin or phantom of a mischievous character, so named from his habit of sitting on bars, or gates. It is said that he can make himself visible in the day time. Rich in the Encyclopaedia Metropolitana relates a story of a lady whom he knew, who had been brought up in a country. She had been passing through the fields one morning when a girl, and saw, as she thought, someone sitting on a stile: however, as she drew near, it vanished.
Candle No. 39; Oil No. 11; Incense No. 4.

BEARDED DEMON:

The demon who teaches the secret of the Philosopher's stone. He is but little known; the demon, barbu, is not to be confused with barbatos, a great and powerful demon who is a duke in Hades, though not a philosopher; nor with Barbas, who is interested in mechanics. It is said that the bearded demon is so called on account of his remarkable beard.
Candle No. 15; Incense No. 8; Oil No. 2.

BECHARD:

A demon alluded to in the key of Solomon as having power over the winds and the tempests.
Candle No. 4; Incense No.5; Oil No. 9.

BELPHEGOR:

The demon of discoveries and ingenious inventions. He appears always in the shape of a young woman. The Moabites, who called him Baalphegor, adored him on Mount Phegor. He it is who bestows riches.
Candle No. 25; Incense No. 1; Oil No. 6.

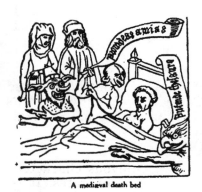

A mediæval death bed

The Trumpeter of Evil

MEDIÆVAL CONCEPTIONS

OF THE DEVIL

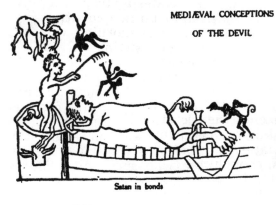

Satan in bonds

The witch and the demon

The Demon of the Treasure

Condemned souls carried to their place of punishment

Beryl:

Beryl, said to preserve wedded love and to be a good medium for magical vision.

Candle No. 38; Incense No. 4; Oil No. 13.

BIFFANT:

A little-known demon, chief of a legion who entered the body of one Denise de la Caile (q. v.) and who was obliged to sign with his claws the proces verbal of exorcisms.

Candle No. 37; Incense No. 7; Oil No. 15.

BUER:

According to Wierius, a demon of the second class. He has naturally the form of a star, and is gifted with a knowledge of philosophy and of the virtues of medicinal herbs. He gives domestic feliticy, and health to the sick. He has charge over fifteen legions.

Candle No. 26; Incense No. 3; Oil No. 12.

BUNE:

According to Wierius a most powerful demon, and one of the Grand Dukes of the Infernal Regions. His form is that of a man. He dose not speak save by signs only. He removes corpses, haunts cemeteries, and marshals the demons around tombs and the places of the dead. He enriches and renders eloquent those who serve him. Thirty legions of the infernal army obey his demanding call. The demons who own his sway called Bunis, are regarded by the Tartars as exceedingly evil. Their power is great and their number immense. But their sorcerers are ever in communication with these demons by means of whom they carry on their dark practices.

Candle No. 27; Incense No. 2; Oil No. 2.

CAACRINOLAAS:

According to Wierius (q. v.) Grand President of Hell also known as Caasimolar and Glasya. He is figured in the shape of a god with the wings of a griffon. He is supposed to inspire knowledge of the liberal arts, and to incite homicides. It is this fiend who can render man invisible. He commands thirty-six legions.

Candle No. 36; Incense No. 9; Oil No. 14.

CACODEMON!

The name given by the ancients to an evil spirit. He changed his shape so frequently that no one could tell in what guise he most generally appeared to man. Each person was also supposed to have a good and bad genuis, the evil being the cacodemon. The astrologers also called the twelfth house of the sun, which is regarded as evil, that of cacodemon.

Candle No. 6; Incense No. 7; Oil No. 3.

CHESME:

A cat-shaped weel-or fountain-spirit or nymph of the Turks. She inveigles youths to death much in the same manner as the Lorelei.

Candle No. 35; Incense No. 8; Oil No. 5.

COUNTS OF HELL:

Demons of a superior order in the infernal hierarchy, who command number of legions. They may be evoked at all hours of the day, provided the evocation takes place in a wild, unfrequented spot.

Candle No. 24; Incense No. 6; Oil No. 1.

CHITON:

An evil spirit.

Candle No. 29; Incense No. 7; Oil No. 5.

DU-SITH or BLACK ELF:

A little man, believed to be of fairy origin, who killed Sir Lachlan Mor M'Clean at the battle of Trai-Gruinard, in Islay, Scotland, in the year 1598. The story runs that this little man offered his services to Sir James Macdonald, the opponent of Sir Lachlan; and that the later's death was caused by an arrow which struck him on the head, and was afterwards found to be an Elf-bolt. In reply to a question of Macdonald's the little man replied: "I am called Du-sith, and you were better to have me with you than against you."

Candle No. 17; Incense No. 3; Oil No. 6.

EBLIS or HARIS:

The "Satan" of the Mohammedans. It is said that he was an inmate of Azazil, the heaven nearest God; and when

the angels were commanded to bow down to the first man, Eblis was the chief of those who rebelled. They were cast out of Azazil, and Eblis and his followers were sentenced to suffer in hell for a long time. It is supposed that he was composed of the elements of fire; and that he succeeded the perils in the government of the world.
Candle No. 4; Incense No. 3; Oil No. 1.

EVERRITT, MRS.:

An English medium who gave private seances so early as 1855. To these sessions were admitted her private friends, and enquirers introduced by them. When a prayer had been said, and the lights turned out the spirits manifested themselves by raps, table-tiltings, lights and spirit voices. Mr. Morell Theobald, a prominent spiritualist, was neighbor and friend to Mr. and Mrs. Everitt, and was first attracted to the subject through their instrumentality.
Candle No. 34; Incense No. 9; Oil No. 1.

FOUNTAIN SPIRTS OF BEHMAN:

According to Jacob Behman, there were in nature seven active principles, the "Fountain Spirits, or "Mothers of Existance." These were—the astrigent quality of fire; the quality of love, the quality of sound; and the quality of essential substance. The reciprocal action of these anti? pathetic qualities resulted in Supreme Unity. Each is at once the parent and the child of all the rest for they generate and are generated by each other. They are typified by the seven golden candlesticks of the Apocalypse.
Candle No. 30; Incense No. 14; Oil No. 3.

GOBLIN:

A spirit formerly supposed to lurk in houses. They were generally of mischievous and grotesque type. Hobgoblins, according to Junius, were so called because they were wont to hop on one leg.
Candle No. 8; Incense No. 10; Oil No. 4.

GRUGACH:

That is "long-haired one," from the Gaelic gruag, a wig; a fairy being with protective duties, to be met with in Scottish legends, and which apparently may be of either

The Demon—Ashtoreth

The Demon—Baal

The Demon—Eurynome

The Demon—Amduscias

The Demon—Asmodeus

The Demon—Belphegof

125

sex. The Gruagach appears to have been particularly associated with cattle, and milk was laid aside for him every evening—otherwise no milk would be got at next milking. Usually this being was of a beneficent nature, although occasionally it showed mischievous traits loosing the cattle in the bryes so that the herds had to get up, sometimes several times during a night, to tie them up; this apparently caused the Gruagach much delight. There are many tales in different part of Scotland about the Gruagach, from which one gathers that this fairy commonly had long hair and was well dressed, of whichever sex it might happen to be .

Candle No. 31; Incense No. 7; Oil No. 2.

HABONDIA:

Queen of the fairies, witches, harpies, furies, and ghosts of the wicked. This definition is according to the statement of Pierre Delancre, in his work on the Inconstancy of Demons.

Candle No. 33; Incense No. 5; Oil No. 14.

HAJOTH HAKADOS:

One of the Spheres of angels, by whose agency Jehovah's providence is spread. The Jews believe that these angels inhabit one of the hierarchies named "Jehovah," and that the simple essence of the divinity flows through the Hajoth Hakados to the angel Ametratton" and to the ministering spirit "Reschith Hajalalim."

Candle No. 9; Incense No. 10; Oil No. 3.

HAM:

A Norwegian storm-fiend in the shape of an eagle with black wings, sent by Helgi to engulf Frithjof as he sailed for the island of Yari Angantyr, in the sage of Grettir.

Candle No. 32; Incense No. 5; Oil No. 6. .

HAYDEN, MRS.:

The first spiritualistic medium to visit England. Mrs. Hayden was the wife of W. B. Hayden, editor of the Star Spangled Banner. Her seance phenomena consisted mainly of raps, by means of which communication with the spirits was established. Her supernormal faculties were testified

to by Professor re Morgan in a letter dated, July, 1853, and by Robert Chambers in Chambers' Journal, May 1853.
Candle No. 15; Incense No. 5; Oil No. 5.

HERNE, J.:

A medium who was associated with Charlee Williams (q. v.) during a part of the latter's career and who afterwards practised on his own account. Materialization was a special feature of his seances. And Miss Florence Cook held her first materialization seance in conjunctions with Herne. He was one of the mediums present on the occasion of Mrs. Gupp's famous transit, and was himself on one occasion transported in like manner.
Candle No. 10; Incense No. 3; Oil No. 1.

HEYD:

A Norwegian sea-witch or storm fiend in the shape of a white bear, alluded to in the saga of Grettir. With the other storm-fiend Ham, she sent Helgi to engulf Frithjof as he sailed for the island of Yari Angantyr.
Candle No. 14; Incense No. 2; Oil No. 11.

HMIN NAT:

An evil spirit.
Candle No. 13; Incense No. 4; Oil No. 13.

HOBGOBLIN, ROBIN GOODFELLOW, or PUCK:

An English domestic fairy or brownie of nocturnal habits. He is of a happy disposition and is believed to be one of those courtiers, probably the jester at the court of Oberon. Reginald Scot, in his Discovery of Witchcraft says "Your grandames' maids were wont to set a bowl of milk for him for his pains in grinding of malt, and mustard, and sweeping the house at midnight. This white bread, and milk was his only feul." He is perhaps best known in Britain by his appellation of Puck, an his qualities and attributes are represented under this name in Shaekspeare's Midsummer's Night's Dream." By some he is believed to be the demon who leads men astray during the night. Sometimes he is clothed in a suit of leather close to his body, and sometimes he wore green. He is usually represented as full of tricks and michief.
Candle No. 11; Incense No. 1; Oil No. 7.

HOCUS POCUS:

Words of magical import, which by some are believed to be derived from "Ochus Bochus" a magician and demon of the north. It is perhaps more probable, however, that as others say they are a corruption of the Latin words "hoc est corpus," and are an imitation of the act of transubstantiation practised by the priests of the Church of Rome.
Candle No. 12; Incense No. 3; Oil No. 5.

HYLE:

The name given by the Ghostics to one of the three degrees in the progress of spirits.
Candle No. 1; Incense No. 2; Oil 7.

IFRITS:

Hideous spectres probably of Arabian origin, now genii of Persian and Indian mythology. They assume diverse forms, and frequent ruins, woods, and wild desolate places, for the purpose of preying upon men and other living things. They are sometimes confounded with the Hinns or Divs of Persia.
Candle No. 5; Incense No. 5; Oil No. 12.

IGNIS FATUSS:

A wavering luminous appearance frequently observed in meadows and marshy places, round which many popular superstitions cluster. Its folknames, Will o' the Wisp and Jack o' Lantern, suggest a country fellow bearing a lantern or straw-torch (wisp). Formerly these lights were supposed to haunte desolate bogs and moorlands for the purpose of misleading travelers, and drawing them to their death. Another superstitution says that they are the spirits of those who have been drowned in the bogs, and yet another, that they are the souls of unbaptized infants. Science refers these ignis fautui to gaseous exhalations from the moist ground, or more rarely, to night-flying insects.
Candle No. 7; Incense No. 10; Oil No. 6.

INCUBUS:

A spirit which has intercourse with mortal women.
Candle No. 6; Incense No. 1; Oil No. 7.

JASPER:

Prevents fever and dropsy, strengthens the brain, and promotes .elquence; it is a preservative against deluxions, the nightmare, and epilepsy, and is often met with in the east as a counter-charm. Marbodaeus mentions seventeen species of this stone, but like "the emerald" it is most noted for its magical virtues.

Candle No. 21; Incense No. 9; Oil No. 5.

JEANNE, D'ARC:

Jeanne d'Arc was born in the village of Domremy, near Vaucouleurs, on the border of Champagne and Lorraine, on Jan. 6, 1412. She was taught to spin and sew, but not to read and write, these accomplishments being unusual and unnecessary to people in her station of life. Her parents were devout, and she was brought up piously. Her nature was gentle, modest and religious; but with no physical weakness or morbidity; on the contrary she was exceptionally strong, as her later history shows. At or about the age of thirteen Jeanne began to exeprience what psychology now calls "auditory hallucinations." In other words, she heard "voices"—usually accompanied by a bright light— when no visible person was present. This, of course, is a common sympton of impending mental disorder; but no insanity developed in Jeanne d'Arc. Starled she naturally was at first; but continuation led to familiarity and trust. The voices gave good counsel of a very commonplace kind, as for instance, that she "must be a good girl and go often to church." Soon, however, she began to have visions; saw St. Michael, St. Catherine, and St. Margaret; was given instructions as to her mission; eventually made her way to the Dauphin, put herself at the head of 6,000 men, and advanced to the relief of Orleans, which was surrounded by the victorious English. After a fortnight of hard fighting, the siege was raised, and the enemy driven off. The tide of war had turned, and in three months the Dauphin was crowned king at Rheims as Charles the Seventh.

At this point, Jeanne felt that her mission was accomplished. But her wish to return to her family was overruled by the king and archbishop, and she took part in further fighting against the allied bravery and tactical skill. But in November, 1430, a desperate sally from Cómpiegne — which was besieged by the Duke of Burgendy—she fell into the enemy's hands, was sold to the English, and thrown into dungeon at their headquarters in Rouen.

After a year's imprisonment she was brought to trial before the Bishop of Beauvais, in an ecclesiastical court. The charges were heresy and sorcery. Learned doctors of the church, subtle lawyers, did their best to entangle the simple girl in their dialectical toils; but she showed a remarkable power of keeping to her affirmations and of avoiding heretical statements. "God has always been my Lord in all that I have done," she said. But the trial was only pretence, for her fate was already decided. She was condemned to the stake. To the end, she solemnly affirmed the reality of her "voices" adding that her depositions were true. Her last word, as the smoke and flame rolled round her, was "Jesus." Said an English soldier, awestruck by the manner of her passing: "We are lost; we have burned a Saint." The idea was corroborated in popular opinion by events which followed, for speedy death—as if by Heaven's anger—overtook her judges and accusers. Inspired by her example and weakening on the side of the enemy, the French took heart once more; and the English were all but swept out of the country.

Jeanne's family was rewarded by ennoblement, under the name of De Lys. Twenty-five years after her death, the Pope acceded to a petition that the process by which she was condemned should be-examined. The result was that the judgment was reversed and her innocence established and proclaimed. The life of the Maid supplies a problem which orthodox science cannot solve. She was a simple peasant girl, with no ambitious hankering after a career. She rebelled pathetically against her mission. "I had far rather rest and spin by mother's side, for this is no work of my choosing but I must go and do it, for my Lord wills it. She cannot be dismissed on the "simple idiot" theory of Voltaire, for her genius in war and her aptitude in repartee undoubtedly proved exceptional mental powers, unschooled though she was in what we call education. We cannot call her a mere hysteric, for her health and strength were superb. It is on record that a man of science said to an Abbe:—"Come to the Salpetriere Hospital, and I will show you twenty Jeannes d'Arc." To which the Abbe responded: "Has one of them given us back Alsace and Lorraine?" The retort was certainly neat. Still, though the Salpetriere hysterics have not won back Alsace and Lorraine, it is nevertheless true that many great movements have sprung from fraud or hallucination. May it not have been so, with Jeanne? She delivered France, and her importance in history is great; but may not her mission and her doings have been the outcome of merely subjective hallucinations, induced by the brooding of her specially religious and patriotic mind on the woes of her country? The army, being ignorant and superstitious, would readily believe in the supernatural nature of her mission, and great energy and valour would result—for a man fights well when he feels that Providence is on his side.

This is the most usual kind of theory in explanation of the facts. But it is not fully satisfactory. How came it—one may ask—that this untotured peasant girl could persuade not only the rude soldiery, but also the Dauphin and the Court, of her Divine appointment? How came she to be given the command of an army? Surely a post of such responsibility and power would not be given to an ignorant girl of eighteen, on heretical strength of her own claim to inspiration.

It seems, at least, very improbable. Now it so happens (though the materialistic school of historians conveniently ignore or belittle it) that there is strong evidence in support of the idea that Jeanne gave the Dauphin some proof of the possession of supernormal faculties. In fact, the evidence is so strong that Mr. Andrew Lang called it "Unimpeachable"—and Mr. Lang did not usually err on the side of credulity in these matters. Among other curious things, Jeanne seems to have repeated to Charles the words of a prayer which he had made mentally and she also made some kind of clairvoyant discovery of a sword hidden behind the altar of Fierbois church. Schiller's magnificent dramatic poem—"Die Junglfrau von Orleans"—though unhistorical in some details, is substantially accurate on these points concerning clairvoyance and mind-reading.

These books on the Maid by Anatole France (two vols.) and Mr. Andrew Lang giving respectively the sceptical and the believing side as to the explanation of her experiences. There is also a very useful little book by Miss C. M. Antony, with preface by Father R. H. Benson.
Candle No. 32; Incense No. 10; Oil No. 1.

JESODOTH:
The angel through which Elohim, the source of knowledge, understanding and wisdom was imparted to the earth. This belief is of Jewish origin.
Candle No. 16; Incense No. 7; Oil No. 5.

JOHN KING:
A spirit.
Candle No. 24; Incense No. 5; Oil No. 12.

KATIE KING:
A spirit.
Candle No. 19; Incense No. 8; Oil No. 3.

KELPIE, THE:
A water spirit, which, in Scotland, is believed to haunt streams and torrents. Kelpies appear to be of a mischievous nature and were often accused of stopping the water-wheels of mills, and of swelling streams. The Kelpie is occasionally used as a name of terror to frighten unruly children; and it was believed that he also devoured women.
Candle No. 17; Incense No. 4; Oil No. 6.

KEVAN of the CURLING LOCKS:
The lover of Cleena who went off to hunt in the woods, leaving her to be abducted by the fairies.
Candle No. 40; Incense No. 3; Oil No. 15.

KHAIB:
The Egyptian name for the shadow, which at death was supposed to quit the body to continue a separate existence of its own. It was represented under the form of a sunshade.
Candle No. 12; Incense No. 2; Oil No. 7.

KHU:

The Egyptian name for one of the immortal parts of man, probably the spirit. The word means "clear" or "luminous" and is symbolised by a flame of fire.
Candle No. 13; Incense No. 9; Oil No. 12.

KOON'S SPIRIT ROOM:

A log seance-room erected in Dover, Athens County, Ohio, by a farmer, Jonathan Koons, in 1852. Koons, an early convert to spiritualism, had been told that he and his eight children would develop mediumistic powers and the spirit-room was intended to be used for manifestations produced by their mediumship. The room was furnished with the appliances incidental to the spiritualistic seance—table for rappings, tambourines, and other musical instruments; phosphorus, by means of which the spirits might show themselves. The phenomena witnessed by the sitters, including Charles Partridge editor of the Spiritual Telegraph were of a varied nature; but in the main identical with the other manifestations of the same period. The spirits who visited KOON'S log building claimed to be a band—one hundred and sixty-five in number—of men that had lived before the time of Adam, and from whom were descended the well-known spirit personalities, John and Katie King.
Candle No. 7; Incense No. 1; Oil No. 9.

KOSTCHTCHIE, or "DEATHLESS"

A Russian goblin of the bogle-boe species. This horrid monster is described as having a death's head and fleshless skelton, "through which is seen the black blood flowing and the yellow heart beating." He is armed with an iron club, with which he knocks down all who come in his path. In spite of his ugliness, he is said to be a great admirer of young girls and women. He is avaricious, hates old and young alike, and particularly those who are fortunate. His dwelling is said to be amongst the mountains of the Keskels and the Caucasus, where his treasure is concealed.
Candle No. 2; Incense No. 1; Oil No. 9.

MID-DAY DEMONS:

The ancients frequently made mention of certain demons who became visible especially towards mid-day to those with whom they had a pact. They appeared in the form of men or of beasts, and let themselves be enclosed in a character, a figure, a vial, or in the interior of a hollow ring.

Candle No. 4; Incense No. 7; Oil No. 13.

NAT:

An evil spirit.

Candle No. 19; Incense No. 6: Oil No. 5.

OBERION:

A spirit.

Candle No. 28; Incense No. 10; Oil No. 12.

PLANTARY SPIRITS:

In the theosophical scheme the number of these spirits is seven. They are emanations from the Absolute, and are the agents by which the Absolute effects all his changes in the Universe.

Candle No. 21; Incense No. 7; Oil No. 6.

RAKSHASA:

An Indian demon. In one of the Indian folktales he appears black as soot, with hair yellow as the lightning, looking like a thunder-cloud. He had made himself a wreath of entrails; he wore a sacrificial cord of astrology, and was the author of several astrological and other works.

Candle No. 6; Incense No. 3; Oil No. 15.

RAPHAEL, THE ANGEL:

In the prophecy of Enoch it is said that: "Raphael presides over the spirits of men." In the Jewish rabbinical legend of the angelic hierarchies Raphael is the medium through which the power of Tsebaoth, or the Lord of hosts, passes into the sphere of the sun, giving motion, heat and brightness to it.

Candle No. 3; Incense No. 8; Oil No. 12.

RED MAN: 6

The demon of the tempests. He is supposed to be furious when the rash voyager intrudes on his solitude, and to show his anger in the winds and storms. The French peas-

ants believed that a mysterious little red man appeared to Napoleon to announce coming reverses.
Candle No. 16; Incense No. 4; Oil No. 14.

RESCHITH HAJALALIM:

The name of the ministering spirit in the Jewish rabbinical legend of the angelic hierarchies. To this angel, the pure and simple essence of the divinity flows through Hajoth Hakakos; he guides the priummobile, and bestows the gifts of life on all.

ROBERT THE DEVIL:

He was the son of a Duke and Duchess of Normandy. He was endowed with marvellous physical strength, which he used only to minister to his evil passions. Explaining to him the cause of his wicked impulses, his mother told him that he had been born in answer to prayers addressed to the devil. He now sought religious advice, and was directed by the Pope to a hermit who ordered him to maintain complete silence, to take his food from the mouths of dogs, to feign madness and to provoke abuse from common people without attempting to retaliate. He became court fool to the Roman Emperor and three times delivered the city from Saracen invasions, having been prompted to fight by a heavenly message. The emperor's dumb daughter was given speech in order to identify the saviour of the city with the court fool, but he refused his due recompense as well as her hand in marriage, and went back to the hermit, his former confessor. The French romance of Robert le Diable is one of the oldest forms of this legened.
Candle No. 31; Incense No. 7; Oill No. 11.

SABBATHI:

To this angel, in the Jewish rabbinical legend of the celestial hierarchies, is assigned the sphere of Saturn. He receives the divine light of the Holy Spirit, and communicates it to the dwellers in his kingdom.
Candle No. 8; Incense No. 3; Oil No. 14.

SPUNKIE:

A goblin of the same nature as the Scottish "Jelpie". He is popularly believed to be an agent of Satan, and travellers who lose their way are his especial prey. He attracts his unfortunate victim by means of a light, which looks as if it were a reflection on a window and is apparently not far away; but as the man proceeds towards it, like the rainbow it recedes. However, he still follows its gleam, until the Spunkie has successfully lured him over a precipice or into a morass.

Candle No. 17; Incense No. 5; Oil No. 12.

VERDELET:

A demon of the second order, master of ceremonies at the infernal court. He takes the names of Master Persil, Sante-Buisson, and other names of a pleasant sound, so as to entice women into his snares.

Candle No. 1; Incense No. 2; Oil No. 6.

ZAEBOS:

A Grand count of the infernal regions. He appears in the shape of a handsome soldier mounted on a crocodile. His head is adorned with a ducal coronet. He is of a gentle disposition.

Candle No. 29; Incense No. 4; Oil No. 9.

ZAGAM:

Grand king and president of the infernal regions. He appears under the form of a bull with the wings of a griffin. He changes water into wine, blood into oil, the fool into a wise man, lead into silver, and copper into gold. Thirty legions obey him.

Candle No. 17; Incense No. 7; Oil No. 11.

ZAPAN:

According to Wierwius, one of the kings of Hell.

Candle No. 19; Incense No. 9; Oil No. 10.

ZEPAR:

Grand duke of the infernal empire, who may be identical with Vepar, or Separ. Nevertheless, under the name of Zepar he has the form of a warrior. He casts men into evil passions. Twenty-eight legions obey him.

Candle No. 2; Incense No. 4; Oil No. 6.

ZEERNEBOOCH:

A dark god, monarch of the empire of the dead among the ancient Germans.

Candle No. 16; Incense No. 7; Oil No. 5.

ZADKIEL:

One of the angels in the Jewish rabbinical legend of the celestial hierarchies. He is the ruler of Jupiter, and through him pass grace, goodness, mercy, piety, and munficence, and he bstows clemency, benevolence and justice to all.

Candle No. 3; Incense No. 6; Oil No. 9.